Fire in the Soul

A Collection of Devotional Messages and Sermon-Starters

"...So the word of the Lord has brought me insult and reproach all day long. But if I say, 'I will not mention him or speak any more in his name,' his word is in my heart like a fire, a fire shut up in my bones. I am weary of holding it in; in deed, I cannot."

\- Jeremiah 20: 8-9

Fire in the Soul

A Collection of Devotional Messages and Sermon-Starters

Jim Biscardi, Jr.

Fire in the Soul
A Collection of Devotional Messages and Sermon-Starters

© 2006 by James Biscardi, Jr.

ISBN 0-9753786-1-9

All Rights Reserved

This document may not be reproduced or transmitted in any form or by any means, electrical, mechanical including photocopying, recording, or any information storage and retrieval system without permission in writing from the publisher.

Published By

Mantle Ministries
PO Box 248
Lanoka Harbor, NJ 08734

Cover design by Faithlyn Robinson
Cover photos by Dreamstime

With much gratitude…

Whenever you decide to write a book, you know that the road is paved with long lonely hours, physical and mental exhaustion, uncaring critics, and writer's block. But there is always one person who persistently keeps encouraging me. My wife, Patty, sees beyond the hard work to those wonderful folk who will take the time to read my books. Knowing she must tread the path of loneliness, herself, and being assured that she will share my time and conversation with a laptop computer, she still encourages me to press on. She sincerely senses when the Holy Spirit is prompting me to be creative, knows that my response to Him must be, "Yes, Lord", and becomes for me a faithful advisor and reliable sounding board. She truly is one with *"Fire in the Soul."* And without her confidence in me, this book would not have been possible. And so my heart felt deepest gratitude and love go out to her.

Fire in the Soul[1]

Is the Spirit glowing in thy heart?
Oh, my brother, can you say
That you feel the burning love of God
In thy bosom day by day?

Has the merit of the blood divine
Swept away thy sinful stain?
And does heaven's glory in Thee shine,
Ever bright and holy flame?

Is thy hope unclouded by a fear?
At this moment do you know
That the love of God is burning clear
In thy heart as white as snow?

Do you feel the mighty, living pow'r,
Filling all thy mortal frame?
And does all thy heart forever pour
Streams of glory to His name?

If thy all is on the altar laid,
Guard it from each vain desire;
When thy soul the perfect price hath paid,
God will send the holy fire.

Refrain:
Yes, 'tis love, 'tis burning love divine,
Filling all my soul's desire;
Oh, how sweet its glories ever shine!
Now I feel the glowing fire.

---

[1] Daniel S. Warner, 1887

TABLE OF CONTENTS

Chapter 1

Re-Kindle Our Faith

My Faith Looks Up to Thee[2]

My faith looks up to thee,
thou Lamb of Calvary,
Savior divine!
Now hear me while I pray,
take all my guilt away,
O let me from this day
be wholly thine!

May thy rich grace impart
strength to my fainting heart,
my zeal inspire!
As thou hast died for me,
O may my love to thee
pure, warm, and changeless be,
a living fire!

While life's dark maze I tread,
and griefs around me spread,
be thou my guide;
bid darkness turn to day,
wipe sorrow's tears away,
nor let me ever stray
from thee aside.

When ends life's transient dream,
when death's cold, sullen stream
shall o'er me roll;
blest Savior, then in love,
fear and distrust remove;
O bear me safe above,
a ransomed soul!

---

[2] *Ray Palmer, 1808-1887*

THE WAR AGAINST CHRIST IN AMERICA

Many of us may not realize that there's a war, bigger than IRAQ, that's raging in our own backyard. It's the battle for minds and hearts – especially of our young people - to embrace an antichrist secularism and culture change in America. The battle lines have been drawn by the American Bar Association, American Civil Liberties Union, Americans United for the Separation of Church and State, People for the American Way Foundation, LAMBDA Legal Defense and Education Fund, National Organization of Women, and many others. Like the Antichrist, the Beast, who will soon become a world leader with similar intentions and attitudes, these organizations (unknowingly) are inspired and empowered by Satan, the author of treachery and deceit.

Can you hear the voice of these Goliaths challenging and daring you to stand against them in the court rooms, public schools, colleges, city hall chapels, media, news and entertainment centers? Are we as motivated and inspired as David, who guarded his father's sheep***? "Your servant has killed the lion and the bear; this uncircumcised Philistine will be like one of them, because he has defied the armies of the living God. The Lord who delivered me from the paw of the lion and the paw of the bear will deliver me from the hand of this Philistine."*** 1 Samuel 17: 36-37. Here are just two campaigns in the battle for our children's souls…

MARRIAGE AND HOMOSEXUALITY. Lobbyists for gay rights are positioning themselves on the battlefield as the champions for "real marriage." This is blatant deception and an obvious effort to counterfeit real marriage. Because the homosexual community is dedicated and committed, they will stop at nothing in pursuit of their radical agenda. In November 2003, the Massachusetts

Supreme Judicial Court handed down a troubling decision - that same-sex couples have a constitutional right to marry. This puts same-sex marriage on the same legal footing as marriage between one man and one woman. San Francisco, New York, and New Jersey have seen the fallout of this ruling with illegal same-sex marriage ceremonies. The "*Religious Freedom and Civil Marriage Protection Act*", to issue marriage licenses to gay and lesbian couples, passed the Senate and Assembly in California in 2005 but was vetoed by the governor.

Because of a small minority of radical homosexual activists, we are drawing ever closer to seeing a dramatic and lasting change in our society, unless we, who believe in the sanctity of marriage, take action and demonstrate to Congress that we want marriage protected! See Romans 1: 26-27.

PLEDGE of ALLEGIANCE. Our faith and freedom is facing a serious challenge. The Justice Department appealed to the Supreme Court of the United States, asking the high court to take the Pledge of Allegiance case in order to reverse the federal appeals court ruling that banned the reciting in schools of the Pledge of Allegiance with the phrase, "One nation under God." On June 14, 2004, the Supreme Court ruled that a California father could not challenge the Pledge of Allegiance, a decision that sidestepped the broader question of the separation of church and state.

We still need the United States Supreme Court to UPHOLD THE CONSTITUTIONALITY of the phrase "under God" that has become a time-honored tradition, an integral part of the Pledge for nearly 50 years.

The stakes in this case are incredibly high. But the opposition is fierce! The executive director of Americans United for Separation of Church and State wrote in a column - that appeared in newspapers nationwide - that the phrase "under God" in the Pledge is "a constant slap in the face." And taking "One nation under God" out of the Pledge is JUST THE BEGINNING! If we lose this case, "In God We Trust" on coins could be the next target, followed by the prayers which open Congress, and every other public expression of faith in God – like GOD BLESS AMERICA! Unprecedented religious discrimination will tear down our freedoms across the country.

That's the outcome these modern-day Goliaths want! THE OUTCOME OF THIS BATTLE WILL DETERMINE OUR RELIGIOUS FREEDOM FOR YEARS TO COME.

So what can we do to win these and other battles?

- Put on the spiritual armor our Lord has provided (Ephesians 6: 10-18) and take a stand for Christ on these issues in the home, workplace, church, and school. Engage opponents with spiritual weapons – not carnal ones. Stay in uniform, wearing the helmet of salvation, the breastplate of righteousness, the belt of truth, and the "good news shoes". Learn how to deflect their blows with the shield of faith, and to use the double-edged sword of the Spirit, the Word of God, to both promote healing and to deliver a death blow to Satan – our unseen, real enemy who comes to steal, kill, and destroy. Remember, ***"They overcame him (Satan) by the blood of the Lamb and the word of their testimony."*** Revelation 12: 11.
- PRAY – PRAY - PRAY
- Stay informed on the issues by receiving updates from organizations like The Center For Reclaiming America or The American Center for Law and Justice
- Join other Christians in letting your Congressional representatives know how you feel through signing petitions, email, telephone calls, and letters.
- Vote for candidates that stand for traditional Christian values.

<u>BY FAITH</u> WIN THE WAR AGAINST CHRIST IN AMERICA

Hebrews 11: 1 says, *"Now faith is being sure of what we hope for and certain of what we do not see."* Verse 6 says, *"And without faith it is impossible to please God, because anyone who comes to him must believe that he exists and that he rewards those who earnestly seek him."* James, the Lord's brother, clarifies our understanding of faith. He says, *"...faith by itself, if it is not accompanied by action, is dead...Show me your faith without deeds, and I will show you my faith by what I do."* See James 2: 17, 18b. So then, another way to define "faith" is: Our <u>response</u> to God's love.

God loves us so much that though we were lost in sin, with Satan leading us in rebellion against God and His work, the Lord gave Himself in the form of His Son, Jesus Christ, to take the penalty of death for us which He, the Righteous Judge, had rightly judged as our sentence. Now "faith" is what we do about that love (i.e. what action we take) – accept Christ, follow Him, and serve Him on earth – or reject Christ and continue in Satan's rebellion.

Back in Hebrews 11, we can now better understand this "faith chapter" as it recaps the deeds of many "men of faith": Noah was warned about things he couldn't yet see, and ***took action*** to build an ark to save himself and his family. Abraham, Isaac, and Jacob ***took action*** to leave their homes to find the place that God promised to their descendents. By faith, Abraham ***took action*** to offer his divinely-conceived son – his only link to the future life promised by God – as a sacrificial lamb. By faith, Moses' parents ***took action*** against the king's edict. Later, Moses, himself, ***took action*** to identify himself with Israel rather than enjoy the pleasures of sin for a short time. And the list goes on. All of them were commended for their response to God's love!

So this then begs the question: "What are *we* doing to respond to God's love?" Many of us are demonstrating our faith by serving Christ in innumerable ways at our homes, churches, workplaces, schoolrooms, and wherever we gravitate. We are making disciples through our testimonies, teaching, and being examples of Christ's values and behaviors. Sometimes our faith finds us in "deep water" where only the Lord's outstretched, wounded and faithful hands clasped with our own keep us from drowning!

With all that said, however, there's something dying within America – the home we love that God has blessed - that needs our faithful response. Can you smell the rotting and decay of our foundational Christian values that have historically made America unique on this planet? In the previous article, I told you about our battle against the "Goliaths" of MARRIAGE & HOMOSEXUALITY and the PLEDGE OF ALLEGIANCE. But there are other "giants" that must be slain by faith involving ABORTION, JUDICIAL NOMINEES, CHRISTIANS AT WORK, and LAWS THAT DISCRIMINATE AGAINST CHRISTIANS. Some day, let it be said that "By faith (insert your name) ***took action*** in prayer, stayed informed on the antichristian issues in America, joined with others in petitioning Congressional representatives, and voted for candidates who stood for Christ's values."

Here are some of the victories of faith that were won in our courtrooms:

The San Diego Unified School District DISCRIMINATED AGAINST A CHURCH ...
... after school officials rejected requests to advertise seminars dealing with parenting and school violence - all because the material contained the name of a religious organization. The U.S. District Court correctly determined that this kind of treatment was not only wrong, but also unconstitutional.

RELIGIOUS DISCRIMINATION against a church in Kern County, CA. New Life Assembly filed a lawsuit in U.S. District Court against Kern County and county leadership because the county charged the church a special hourly usage fee totaling $450 to use county-owned property for religious events. County policy dictated no such charge for other non-profit groups. Kern County has entered into a settlement and agreed to reimburse the church and change their policy.

EQUALITY FOR STUDENTS WHO PARTICIPATE IN RELIGIOUS CLUBS on campus. Two students who attend Monarch High School in Louisville, Colorado, were denied permission to form a Bible club although the school district permitted the formation of several other student groups including the Multicultural Club, Peace Jam, Amnesty International, and the Gay/Straight Alliance. After the suit was filed, the school district changed its policy. A settlement agreement acknowledges the new policy permitting religious clubs to meet and guarantees equality for all religious student clubs.

In 2003, the PRESIDENT SIGNED THE PARTIAL-BIRTH ABORTION BAN ACT. The fight for life, however, continues. The pro-abortion lobby has filed suit challenging the ban. By faith, we must stand ready to defend the ban in court.

The Supreme Court of the United States upheld the constitutionality of the Children's Internet Protection Act (CIPA), which mandates any public library that refuses to install Internet filtering software on its computers would become ineligible for federal funds for technology upgrades. This landmark decision marks the first time the Supreme Court has upheld a restriction on pornography on the Internet.

A federal district court judge has ruled that an agency acted unconstitutionally when it suspended a teacher's aide for wearing a cross pendant to school in Pennsylvania. This decision sends a strong message that laws and policies resulting in religious discrimination are not acceptable. This is an important First Amendment victory!

A three-judge panel of a federal appeals court unanimously ruled that the actions of an Arizona school district were discriminatory and unconstitutional when it refused to allow the distribution of literature promoting an event because it contained religious speech. In its decision, the court said the school district's exclusion of the brochures "constitutes impermissible viewpoint discrimination."

"...take up the shield of faith, with which you can extinguish all the flaming arrows of the evil one." Ephesians 6:16.

TRUST AND OBEY – IS THERE NO OTHER WAY?

Do you remember when Jesus said, "When you've seen me, you've seen the Father?" (John 14:9). A big reason for Him to become one of us and walk among us was to show us the Father – to help us know and "hug" our Father – with whom we had broken trust because of sin. As we live and serve our Father, our lives are to reflect Christ. When people see us, they should see the Father. I've been wondering if that's the way it should be between pastors and church members. Should we be saying, "When you see me, you see my pastor?"

Reba Rebel *was not easily led. She was self-motivated and an independent thinker. She was a Sunday School teacher and leader of a Christian school connected to the church. Her ideas required the pastor to change his plans at times to accommodate her "out of the box" thinking. Many of her ideas were successful in motivating people to leave their comfort zones and reach out to the community. She didn't have much money, but she was a gifted, talented person. Reba Rebel, however, could be over-zealous about her ideas. When the pastor and board refused her proposal for new computers in the school, she threatened and eventually left her leadership position. Though a new leader was found, many innovations that Reba Rebel could have instituted were lost forever because she couldn't compromise.*

Young's Compact Bible Dictionary says that the words for **obey** carry also the idea of "hearing." The two concepts are inseparable. The Hebrew "shama" means both "to listen to" and "obey," as does the Greek word "hupakouo." The biblical concept is, then, of a hearing that takes place and the need to comply with what is heard. The child hears and obeys his parents, the pupil his teachers, the employee his employer, the church member his leader. All mankind hears God and is expected to obey (Exodus 19:5; Colossians 3:20, 22). Another Hebrew word is also translated in the NIV as "obey." Its basic meaning is "to guard." As in Psalm 119: 8, "I will (guard) thy statutes.." So with reference to **obeying** those who have the rule over us, there are two responses – to listen and to guard carefully what is said.

I've seen church members ambush the pastor by refusing to submit to his decisions. They also try to maneuver their pastor in several ways. One way is by holding back their tithe. When this happens we are not disobeying the pastor but God, Himself. "Will a man rob God? Yet ye have robbed me. But ye say, Wherein have we robbed thee? In tithes and offerings. Ye are cursed with a curse: for ye have robbed me…Bring ye all the tithes into the storehouse…And I will rebuke the devourer for your sakes and he shall not destroy the fruits of your ground…" (Malachi 3: 10-11). So, the enemy of our soul knows that by refusing to give our tithe to the church, we will ambush ourselves.

Another way church members try to maneuver their pastor is by holding back their time and talents that are needed by the church. This tactic, however, may hurt the pastor, but it primarily is disobedience to God and hurtful to the rest of the congregation. Everyone in the Body of Christ has been given gifts to bless others with – they are not given to the individual but are given *through* an individual to the whole church (1 Corinthians 12:7). We are actually "stealing" from the church and rebelling against God when we don't use the talents He gives us. Ephesians 4:16 NIV tells us that exercising those talents are necessary for the church to grow, " From him the whole body, joined and held together by every supporting ligament, grows and builds itself up in love, *as each part does its work."*

"Obey them that have the rule over you, and submit yourselves: for they watch for your souls, as they must give an account, that they may do it with joy, and not with grief: for that is unprofitable for you." (Hebrews 13:17)

"Remember your leaders, who spoke the word of God to you. Consider the outcome of their way of life and imitate their faith. Jesus Christ is the same yesterday, today, and forever. Do not be carried away by all kinds of strange teachings." (Hebrews 13:7 NIV)

I must also say, however, that the pastor must know there are limits to his authority – otherwise he could ambush his people and lead them into error. As Ruth Graham has said in Decision Magazine, February 2001, "At times we all need to be disagreed with. When someone gets into a position of political or social power or a position of fame or fortune, and when no one dares to disagree, look out! That person is in danger. Someone once gave me a gem of wisdom, 'Where two people agree on everything, one of them is unnecessary.' We can disagree without being disagreeable." We are to follow the pastor *as he follows Christ.* The Apostle Paul said, "Be ye followers of me, even as I also am of Christ." (1 Corinthians 11:1). We are not to trust in the flesh - not ours and not the pastor's. We are "to trust in God with all our heart and lean not on our own understanding." (Proverbs 3:5)

If pastors and church members do their part, we will reflect each other. More importantly, we will also reflect Christ and draw others to Him (John 17:21).

REACH!

Those who read my books and articles realize that I have certain strong beliefs. One of these strong beliefs is in God's weight reduction plan – His spiritual vitamins for reducing the flesh (the natural man) and shaping us in the image of Jesus Christ. Those vitamins are: Prayer, Worship (with lots of gratitude), Fellowship, Study of God's Word, Service, and Comforting Others with the comfort God uses to comfort us through our trials/suffering.

These vitamins help us surrender ourselves as living sacrifices to God and to *"not conform any longer to the pattern to this world but be transformed by the renewing of (our) mind."* See Romans 12: 2. They give us the vigor to emulate Christ and run in His footsteps. They allow us to obey God's command to Abraham: *"I am the Almighty God; walk before me, and be thou perfect."* (Genesis 17:1). We need to be perfectly weak in the flesh so our Lord can work through us and get the glory in our achievements.

Remember Paul's words in 2 Corinthians 12:10, *"Therefore, I will boast all the more gladly about my weaknesses, so that Christ's power may rest upon me. That is why for Christ's sake, I delight in weaknesses, in insults, in hardships, in persecutions, in difficulties. For when I am weak, then I am strong."* As you probably know, of all the apostles, it seems Paul had the most trials and sufferings. These are never easy to navigate through, but knowing that our Lord is with us, and that He uses them to shape and conform us to the image of Christ, helps a lot.

Once again, those who know me, know that my most difficult times come when I am *ambushed* by a brother or sister in Christ through anger, envy, slander, pride, a competitive spirit, and other works of the flesh. Maybe you – like me – have been "wounded by friendly fire" in the local church. Remember, Jesus also endured that same trial for our sakes and also to please His heavenly Father. Some day, when Jesus returns, they will ask Him how He got those wounds in His hands. Scripture tells us that He will answer, ***"Those with which I was wounded in the house of my friends."*** See Zechariah 13:6. In spite of any hurts, I want to encourage you to keep doing what is right – seeking God's kingdom and His righteousness – taking your spiritual vitamins – walking with King Jesus, who is the Lamb upon the throne. In short, keep **REACHING**...

Reach Out To Christ – *"Put your finger here; see my hands. Reach out your hand and put it into my side. Stop doubting and believe."* John 20:27

Reach Out To One Another – *"I tell you the truth, whatever you did for one of the least of these brothers of mine, you did for me."* Matthew 25:40

Reach Out To The Lost – *"...go and make disciples of all nations, ...and teaching them to obey everything I have commanded you."* Matthew 28:19, 20

Reach Higher – *"For as the heavens are higher than the earth, so are my ways higher than your ways, and my thoughts than your thoughts."* Isaiah 55:9

Reach Deeper – *"The Spirit searches all things, even the deep things of God."* 1 Corinthians 2:10

Reach Ahead – *"Forgetting those things that are behind, and reaching forth unto those things that are before..."* Philippians 3:13

Reach Our Goal – *"I press on toward the goal to win the prize (i.e Christ) for which God has called me heavenward in Christ Jesus."* Philippians 3: 8,14

You may be interested to know that the Holy Spirit is leading some of us (e.g. New Jersey Christian Ministries) along new paths to encourage Christians in local churches by providing expert instruction and resources. The goal is to come along side the local church and help better equip members for making disciples. We are forming interdenominational partnerships with pastors, who want their people to keep **REACHING** and providing them access to experts in ministry – over 90 instructors, half with PhDs or who are clergy, and most others who are heads of their own ministries. We are forming Christian **Re**newal **a**nd **Ch**allenge (**REACH**) Centers in churches.

So keep being the faithful servants God wants you to be wherever He has set you in the local church. **REACH** for your life! Pray the words of Adelaide Pollard, "Have Thine own way Lord. Have Thine Own Way. Thou art the Potter. I am the clay. Mold me and make me after Thy will, while I am waiting, yielded and still."

CHRIST'S COMING TO EARTH "PART 2"

Every time we celebrate Christmas, the day of Christ's Second Coming is one year closer! In the fullness of time, Christ will return with His saints (us) to recover the earth and set up world rule. Catch a glimpse of our ultimate victory with Christ from the brief description that follows...

We are told that *"the wedding of the Lamb has come, and his bride has made herself ready."* Revelation 19: 7. How does the bride make herself ready? The Church is the bride of Christ. That includes those of us who are "snatched away" by Jesus in the rapture of the Church. *"...the dead in Christ will rise first. After that, we who are alive and are left will be caught up with them in the clouds to meet the Lord in the air. And so we will be with the Lord forever."* 1 Thessalonians 4: 16-17.

Then comes the Judgment Seat of Christ when each of us *"receives what is due him for the things done while in the body, whether good or bad."* 2 Corinthians 5: 10. That will be a time of both weeping and great joy. Weeping happens when Christians (i.e. the bride) are "uncovered" by Christ as in a biblical Jewish wedding how the bridegroom "uncovers" his wife. I believe we will see missed opportunities and times we acted in our own flesh rather than by God's Spirit. But Christ's warm smile will dry all our tears! Great joy happens when Christ gives us our *"crown of rejoicing"* and "uncovers" the righteous acts of the saints. I believe our crowns will contain people to whom we faithfully witnessed or touched in some way for Christ and, in turn, all the ones they brought to Christ. 1 Thessalonians 2: 19. That's how the bride "makes herself ready."

After the Judgment Seat, comes the marriage supper of the Lamb. Knowing our Lord, He will serve us at that banquet – as much as we will want to serve Him, then as now, we shall never be able to "out give" the Lord. And immediately after this wondrous "love feast", we swiftly find ourselves ready for battle – the final battle for righteousness! The bride was granted that *"she be arrayed in fine linen, clean and bright, for the fine linen is the righteous acts of the saints."* John sees heaven opened (Revelation 19: 11-21) and Christ, with many crowns (i.e. those we cast at His feet – Revelation 4:10), is seated upon a white horse. His name is called Faithful and True, the Word of God. On His thigh is written, KING OF KINGS and LORD OF LORDS. Revelation 19: 16. And all the redeemed saints, described as *"the armies in heaven clothed in fine linen, white and clean"*, follow Him on white horses back to earth for the battle of Armageddon. John records that he saw the beast (i.e. Antichrist) and the kings of the earth, and their armies gathered together to make war against Him that sat on the horse and His army. Revelation 19: 19.

Every eye shall see Him and His entourage. We will be all aglow, shining like stars, (Daniel 12:3) with the Sun of Righteousness leading us. We'll look like billions of smaller stars flowing behind Christ forming His mantle. Then, what God told Abraham, Isaac, and Jacob about their descendents being as innumerable as the stars of heaven will become literally true. Remember His words to Abraham, *"Look now toward heaven, and tell the stars, if thou be able to number them: and he said unto him, So shall thy seed be."* Genesis 15:5.

Revelation 19:15 then says, *"And out of his mouth goeth a sharp sword, that with it he should smite the nations: and he shall rule them with a rod of iron: and he treadeth the winepress of the fierceness and wrath of Almighty God."* The sword (i.e. the spoken word) that proceeds out of Christ's mouth is two-edged. It can bring life or kill. He spoke the word and His friend Lazarus, who was dead four days, came to life again. John 11:38-44. In a short while (Revelation 20:4) Christ will resurrect those who were beheaded for their testimony of Christ, who did not receive the mark of the Beast. We are told about Christ, *"In the beginning was the Word, and the Word was with God, and the Word was God. He was with God in the beginning. Through him all things were made; without him nothing was made that has been made. In him was life..."* John 1:1-4.

As the Alpha and Omega, He is the beginning and ending of life itself. In the verses that follow, we see the other edge of that sword as Christ's word brings death. *Then the beast was captured, and with him the false prophet who worked signs in his presence, by which he deceived those who received the mark of the beast and those who worshiped his image. These two were cast alive into the lake of fire burning with brimstone. And the rest were killed with the sword which proceeded from the mouth of Him who sat on the horse.* Revelation 19: 20-21. Satan will be chained up. Our Lord will then separate the nations as He describes in Matthew 25:31-46 and His thousand-year reign begins on earth with us ruling and reigning with Him.

This description of Christ's coming stands in sharp contrast to His first arrival on earth as a baby destined to give His life for the sin of the world. There's still time to accept Him as Savior and Lord. There's still time to be part of His returning army. For us Christians, we're like the virgins awaiting the bridegroom. Some are wise. They diligently prepare themselves for the Master's coming, heeding the call to grow in the grace and knowledge of the Lord. 2 Peter 3: 18; 1: 5-8. Some are foolish. They know the Lord is coming, but they are not prepared. Are we like the wise virgins or the foolish ones? Matthew 25: 1-13.

HOW WOULD YOU ANSWER THESE QUESTIONS?

- **How can a loving God allow such cruel things to happen?** Because God loves us, He made man with a free will. We are not puppets manipulated by God. Man needs to choose to be God's child of his own free will. Satan inspires people to do cruel things as they choose to obey him instead of God. These people, however, can become Christ's. As we take a stand for Christ, we take more of the "kingdoms of this world" back for God – then there is less crime.
- **Why does God allow deformed or brain damaged babies to be born?** I believe it is because God wants other people to see them and consider how blessed they are – saying, "There but for the grace of God go I". In addition, He uses these babies – the weak things of the world – to confound the wise. I've know a Down's Syndrome man for 25 years. He's perfect. He's loved by all and shows pure, unconditional love to everyone he meets.
- **Why didn't God heal my friend from cancer?** God's ways are not our ways. His thoughts are higher than our thoughts. Though we see things as tragedies, God may have something even more wonderful than we can imagine for the one who goes to be with him. Children who die are automatically with Him. When someone dies without receiving Christ, this should move Christians to "press toward the finish line" more intensely, and to love the unsaved more practically, drawing them to Christ.
- **Why do good people suffer for what appears to be no reason?** For Christians the example is Christ. When we take a stand for Him, we make enemies. Jesus said that He came not to bring peace but rather division. People must choose Him as

the only way to the Father or not. The persecution fallout of Him being the "Only Way" impacts all Christians.

- **Why didn't God just eliminate Satan in the Garden of Eden?** God created man to have fellowship with Him – to be His children and obey Him – by their freewill choice. God was broken-hearted over man's sin and our broken relationship with Him. So He sent Christ to demonstrate His great sacrificial love for us, to satisfy the penalty for sin, and heal the broken relationship. Man needs to choose Christ. God allows Satan to exist so we make a choice (i.e. Him and eternal life or the temporary gratification in this life and eternal death). We choose now either the "riches in glory by Christ Jesus" or the riches that the world system and Satan give.
- **Why do the wicked seem to get their way and prosper?** Just like Jesus was tempted in the wilderness, Satan also tempts many to "worship him" in order to get power, influence, riches, and gratification of the human nature and the "old man". That's why the devil is called the god of this world and the power of the air.
- **Why did God allow the "old man" to put us in bondage to sin?** It was not God, but man, who put himself into bondage by disobeying God's command. God then used that to show us how much He loves us by sending Jesus to die for us and to crucify the "old man" (RO 6:6) in us. So man could then choose to be His voluntarily.
- **Why do some come to Christ when they hear the gospel and others don't? Does God stop some from receiving Christ?** God has foreknowledge of those who will come to Him – that's because He is God and knows everything past, present, and future. He desires, however, that <u>all</u> come to Christ (JN 3:16). The world and Satan seem to have a hold more on some than on others. I've heard that most people come to Christ when they are young because they can accept change easier than older people. Jesus said that after people have tasted the "old wine" they like it better than the new, referring to the difficulty to accept new truth (LK 5:39). It's also true that some have

more fertile "soil" for the Gospel than others – because of the "planting and watering" of others.

- **How can I prove that Christ rose from the dead (and hence that He is the Son of God)?** The best book on this subject is ***"More Than a Carpenter"*** by Josh McDowell. First, the best way to convince others is by the change in your own life. Remember that we defeat the enemy by the "blood of the Lamb and the word of our testimony." Here is more help:
    - **Theory – Jesus never died.** Answer – How could a bleeding, wounded, and eventually dead Messiah have inspired the fearful disciples to gain such great confidence to the point of giving up their own lives for Christ?
    - **Theory – The disciples moved His body.** Answer – It's unbelievable that this band of fearful men and women could have overpowered or tricked the Roman soldiers. If that happened, why wouldn't the guards have hunted down the disciples, punished them, and produced the body of Christ?
    - **Theory – The disciples lied about the resurrection.** Answer – Why then didn't anyone produce Christ's body and show that it was a lie. That would have ended Christianity forever!
    - **Theory – The guards fell asleep and the disciples stole the body.** Answer – That would have been instant death for the guards. These were disciplined soldiers of Rome, who had conquered many people. That didn't happen with undisciplined men.
- **Is it true that all Christians are supposed to prosper financially?** Jesus said, *"Seek ye first the kingdom of God and his righteousness and all these things (i.e. our necessities) will be added unto you"* (MT 6:33). As illustrations He used a lily and the birds – not kings and palaces. In fact, He said that even Solomon, with all his glory, was not dressed as well as the lily. In MAL 6: 10, God says that as we tithe, He will *"open the windows of heaven and pour out a blessing that there shall not be room enough to receive it."* I usually tell people who expect a lot of money because of that scripture to count all their

blessings and see that it is really true – but not necessarily money.

- **Why doesn't God just let someone in church win the lottery so all the church's needs will be met?** God wants everyone to contribute enough of their time, talents, strength, and money so that no need goes unmet in the church. It's the Acts 2: 42-47 solution. He also wants people to learn and build their character into Christ's through working for a living.

TRUSTING THE LORD IN OUR TRIALS

"But I trusted in Thee, O Lord: I said Thou art my God. My times are in thy hand: deliver me from the hand of mine enemies, and from them that persecute me. Make thy face to shine upon thy servant: save me for thy mercies' sake." Psalm 31: 14-16. Here, David is showing his confidence in God and craving His help. We too can trust our Precious Savior's strong, compassionate, nail-pierced, and resurrected hands to keep us in our hour of suffering.

There is no trial or temptation we undergo that isn't common to other men and women. God is always faithful and will not allow us to be tempted above what we are able to bear. He will always provide a way to escape so that we'll be able to bear it. 1 Corinthians 10:13. The Apostle Peter said that the trial of our faith through the pressures of life is much more precious than of gold that is tried in the fire. 1Peter 1:7. Just like the goldsmith knows when he sees his image in the gold that it is purified and ready, our Father wants to see His Son's image in us. He is careful to make the fire hot enough but not too hot to break the vessel. 1 Peter 4:12-13 says, *"Beloved, think it not strange concerning the fiery trial which is to try you, as though some strange thing happened unto you: But rejoice, in as much as ye are partakers of Christ's sufferings; that when his glory shall be revealed, ye may be glad also with exceeding joy."* As a fine jeweler, He is "cutting" the stones perfectly to create the precious jewels that are the foundation of His "showcase city" – the New Jerusalem. Revelation 21:19-20.

Esther Kerr Rusthoi reminds us in her song "When We See Jesus" that all the trials and suffering will be worth it all: "It will be worth it all when we see Jesus. Life's trials will seem so small when we see Christ; One glimpse at His dear face, all sorrow will erase, So bravely run the race till we see Christ." In another song by someone who knew the skillful Potter, we sing "Thank You Lord, for the trials that come my way. In that way I can grow each day as I let you lead. And I thank You Lord for the patience those trials bring. In that process of growing I can learn to care." Lexicon Music, Inc.

He never leaves us alone during our trials. He is an ever-present comfort through them all. 2 Corinthians 1: 3 - 5 explains what God does to teach us caring with the trials and suffering we experience. *"Praise be to the God and Father of our Lord Jesus Christ, the Father of compassion and the God of all comfort, who comforts us in all our troubles, so we can comfort those in any trouble with the comfort we ourselves have received from God."*

When you pour water into a glass, the glass overflows with water. But when suffering is poured into the Christian's life, over time the Holy Spirit performs a miracle in our lives. Instead of the bitterness, anger, and self-pity that suffering could cause pouring out of the Christian, the comfort of God that comforted us during our trials overflows from us to others who are hurting. That may take the form of comforting words, a hug, a kiss, and sometimes just helping them cry. Jesus showed us (e.g. with Mary and Martha when Lazarus died) that He wants us to share in another's sorrow.

It's our very personal relationship to our heavenly Father through Jesus Christ that gets us through trials and helps us allow the Holy Spirit to use them to benefit us and others. Romans 12: 1-2 encourages us to consider it our reasonable service to surrender to God as living sacrifices and let Him transform us into the image of Christ – to let Him reduce the competitor to Christ in us (i.e. our natural man) to zero. This is like Jacob wrestling with the Angel (i.e. Christ) at Peniel. Genesis 32: 24-30. The Lexicon Music songwriter again captures our response to this training: "But it goes against the way I am to put my human nature down, and let the Spirit take control of all I do. Cause when the trials come, my human nature shouts the thing to do. And God's soft prompting can be easily ignored."

As we run the Christian race, we can become at times so hunkered down by our problems that we lose proper perspective. Our problems look big and the power of God looks small. At those times, we need to draw close to our Father and let Him minister to us as He does in Isaiah 40:15, 22. God reminds us in these scriptures that He is much bigger than the world He created.

The eagle, when it senses a storm approaching, flies to the highest peak it can find and waits. When the storm arrives, it extends its wings and lets the wind take it safely above the storm. Similarly, God ministers to us, directs our actions, and gets us through the storms of life. He says, *"But they that wait upon the Lord shall renew their strength; they shall mount up with wings as eagles; they shall run, and not be weary; and they shall walk and not faint."* Isaiah 40:31.

Remember the three Hebrews who were thrown into the fire for not worshipping the image of gold made by Nebuchadnezzar. The Babylonian king said, *"I see four men loose, walking in the midst of the fire, and they have no hurt; and the form of the fourth is like the Son of God."* Daniel 3:25. We're never in the fire alone. Romans 8: 28 tells us, *"All things work together for good to those that love God and are called according to His purposes."*

Our training through trials helps us all stay fit. Spiritually over weight and flabby Christians cannot fulfill their responsibilities to our Lord and our brothers and sisters in Christ. We can and must say with David, "*My times are in thy hand."*

GO AND MAKE DISCIPLES OF ALL NATIONS

Every believer is commissioned by our Lord Jesus Christ to go and make disciples. He said, *"All power is given unto me in heaven and in earth. Go ye therefore, and teach all nations, baptizing them in the name of the Father, and of the Son, and of the Holy Ghost: Teaching them to observe all things whatsoever I have commanded you: and, lo, I am with you always, even unto the end of the world."* (MT 28: 18-20)

Have you ever thought of the Christian life as running a race – God's way? I've been thinking about it that way. And also thinking about the wonderful people God used along the "track" to help me mature in Christ. You know that to disciple others effectively, we must *"lay aside every weight and the sin which doth so easily beset us, and...run with patience the race that is set before us..."* (HE 12: 1). Runners use weights in practice to get ready for the race. It's harder to run that way but it "feels so good" when the weights come off for the real race. Weights are OK in practice, but only hold us back in the real contest. We are in a real race – not practice.

Sin is a weight that prevents us from running our best. As we live the Christian life, we will sin. These sins could become like trying to run a race with an elastic band wrapped around our feet. God, however, knew this and provided a way to lift that weight so we can run patiently all the way to the finish line with His strength and endurance. *"If we confess our sins, he is faithful and just to forgive us our sins, and to cleanse us from all unrighteousness."* (1JN 1:9)

As Christians, we need to keep ourselves pure (1TI 5:22). Entering into a close relationship with evil will corrupt a Christian. Partnering in business or in marriage with an unbeliever is contrary to God's Word (2COR 6:14-15). Remaining pure under these conditions and trying to change the unbeliever could be compared to preventing a muddy river from polluting a clear stream when they meet. Now, having said this, it does not mean that we separate ourselves from unbelievers – on the contrary, these are the very ones who need us most of all. These are the ones (among whom we were a part) that Jesus came to save. He said that the "sick" are the ones who really need a physician. But He also said that though we were in the world, we were not "of the world." So as we run the race with Christ as our Partner and Coach, we cannot at the same time run with the world (AMOS 3:3). We cannot serve two masters – God and the world.

We need to keep the channel between us and our heavenly Father and also our fellow runners continuously free from the obstructions that sin creates. Therefore, we must develop an intimacy with God that allows us to readily confess our sins to Him. This will keep us effective in reaching out and "touching" others – both believers and unbelievers. We need to realize that this is the only race in which spectators get into the race because of the way they see runners running! This is sometimes called "reproducing ourselves": *"And the things thou hast heard of me among many witnesses, the same commit thou to faithful men, who shall be able to teach others also."* (2TI 2:2). These "spectators", who are being molded by the Holy Spirit as they see our lives, are (among others) fellow church members, our children, grandchildren, coworkers, friends, students, team members, or our spouses.

Here are some of my fellow runners – role models who emulated Christ - who mentored me and helped me "press toward the goal to win the prize"...

Mr. Tract was a co-worker who considered his brightest moment the time when he could afford to have a Christian sandwich sign made. It had scriptures on it and Mr. Tract wore it around him as he witnessed and handed out tracts in lower Manhattan. I learned how to be content and how to serve the Lord with gladness.

Mr. Word went to be with the Lord at the age of 99. He got up early every morning and took a cab to work at a gas station till he was 95. He attended my Sunday school class till he couldn't get a ride. Mr. Word would always share words to live by with me as we sat together in church. He taught me to love, appreciate, and study the Word of God.

Ms. Cross taught me to "cross myself out" every morning and be available for service.

Mr. Rich allowed his apartment, where he lived with his wife and three children, to be used to start a church. He was always encouraging me despite his poor circumstances. He showed me how to build loyalty and build up other people – and also how to pray.

Ms. Love lost a child in a horrible accident, her husband had a debilitating disease, and her grandson had an emotional problem. Her major concern – despite all that – was showing the love of Christ to others. She showed me how to speak the truth in love, how to put others first, and how to laugh in the Lord.

Mr. Friend mentored me in leadership. He didn't hesitate to admonish me to keep him on track and to warn me about making certain decisions for my life.

Ms. Wise helped to keep me as gentle as a dove but also as wise as a serpent concerning people using and abusing me.

Mr. Care's wife had cancer. He kept bringing her to one healing service after another until the Lord healed her. At 70 years old this loving servant of the Lord had no pension from the churches he had served over the years. But he kept preaching the Word, as well as visiting and comforting the sick. He taught me all about perseverance and love.

Ms. Sunday was more faithful than most in attending Sunday school. She showed me how everybody can learn and be creative with a little love and encouragement.

Ms. Persevere had a disabled child. This child required much patience and care. Despite this, she ran the race of life God's way by serving the needs of others in and outside the church. She taught me what patient endurance really meant.

THE REASON FOR THE HOPE THAT IS IN US

When we are "born-again", we are "saved" from the spiritual death sentence that God has imposed on those who sin, which includes everyone: *"For the wages of sin is death; but the gift of God is eternal life through Jesus Christ our Lord"*. (Romans 6:23). Both the Old and New Testaments teach that there is life after death. The patriarchs, the psalmists, the prophets, all pointed to the future. In Hebrews we read that Abraham looked *for "a city...whose builder and maker is God."* (Hebrews 11:10) In 2Corinthians 5:1, Paul wrote of *"a building of God, an house not made with hands, eternal in the heavens."* In Genesis 5:24, Enoch *"walked with God: and he was not for God took him."* The Bible tells us that Elijah was taken up to heaven in a chariot of fire. (2 Kings 2:11) The most powerful reason, however, for believing about life after death is the resurrection of Christ. It was witnessed by hundreds (1Corinthians 15:3-7). Though we sense in ourselves that life must be more than just our existence here, Jesus proved once for all that there is life after death.

The resurrection gives meaning to the cross. The death of Christ is terrible news if it ends there. But because of His resurrection, it is "good news" – called "the Gospel". It assures us that His work is finished – that Christ atoned for everyone's sins. It also assures us that His work was perfect and that God was satisfied with His sacrifice – that Jesus was the "propitiation" for our sins. God demonstrated His satisfaction and confirmed Christ's work on the cross to atone for sin by raising Him from the dead (Acts 13:32-33).

Jesus said, *"I am the resurrection, and the life: he that believeth in me though he were dead, yet shall he live: And whosoever that liveth and believeth in me shall never die."* (John 11:25-26).

Salvation for you and me only requires our *repentance* of what *we* have done and our *acceptance* of what ***Christ*** has done for us. We "call upon the name of the Lord." God hears the cry of our repentant heart for forgiveness and "remembers" the work of His Son on our behalf. Our name is then written in heaven in the Lamb's book of ***life***. (Luke 10:20; Revelation 21:27)

When we are "born-again", we are not only "saved" from the death sentence, but also delivered from the power of sin, itself. We are no longer in bondage to serve sin. We are set free to seek the kingdom of God and His righteousness. The "old man" in us that made us slaves to sin – that caused us to enjoy sinning – that convinced us that there was nothing wrong with what we were doing – is crucified with Christ (Romans 6:6). God, sending His Holy Spirit to dwell within us, gives us the power to overcome the temptation and attraction of sin and instead to produce pure "fruit". *"For when ye were servants of sin, ye were free from righteousness. What fruit had ye then in those things whereof ye are now ashamed? For the end of those things is death. But now being made free from sin, and become servants of God, ye have your fruit unto holiness, and the end everlasting life."* (Romans 6:20-22). *"...greater is He that is in you, than he that is in the world."* (1John 4:4). That doesn't mean that we never sin – because our natural man is still alive in us. It means, however, that when we sin the Holy Spirit is faithful to convict us – so that we want to tell God we're sorry for it. And then because of Christ's sacrifice for our sin, *"He (can now be and) is faithful and just to forgive our sins and to cleanse us from all unrighteousness"* (1John 1:9).

There was a missionary who was translating the Bible into a foreign language. He was struggling over the word for "believe". One day a *runner* brought a message to the missionary's camp. He was totally exhausted, found a hammock nearby and collapsed into it. He uttered a phrase that expressed simultaneously his weariness and his contentment at finding a delightful place to relax. They were words that the missionary had never heard before so he asked one of the natives to explain them. It turned out that the runner was saying that he was at the end of himself and was therefore resting all his weight in the hammock. The missionary then realized that these words correctly described what it meant to "believe." To "believe" accurately means that we must first admit that we are sinners and can't help save ourselves – we're at the end of ourselves. Then we must turn from our sin and cast ourselves totally and unreservedly on Christ for salvation.

FAITH is simply taking God at His word…**F**orsaking **A**ll **I** **T**rust **H**im.

Salvation is like the young woman who was brought before the judge for sentencing after committing a crime. The judge issued the verdict after hearing all the evidence. He found her guilty and sentenced her to death – because the crime was deserving of the death sentence. The judge, however, cared very much for this woman because she was his daughter. So he pronounced the sentence but also pronounced that he would trade places with the woman and would suffer the penalty for her – she was spared because the judge accepted the sentence of death for her. The judge was executed for his daughter. Justice was accomplished but the judge showed the young woman great mercy. Similarly, at the cross when Christ was crucified for you and me, justice and mercy "embraced" and we were set free from the death sentence; while God, in the form of His Son, accepted the just punishment.

When we are born-again, we have a "personal" relationship to Jesus Christ – because we have received Him and become children of God (John 1:12). We also have a personal relationship to others who have received Jesus. As in any relationship, the two who are related make time to keep themselves close. The primary ways to have intimacy with God, and keep this personal relationship current and vibrant are prayer, worship, study of God's Word – the Bible, fellowship with other born-again believers, and surrendering to God for service.

"PERFECTLY WEAK" TO SERVE

All of God's prophets wore a mantle (or some translations call it a cloak). It was a sleeveless garment made from the skin of an animal with the hair left on it. It was the symbol or badge of their office. As the mantle "served" the prophet, we as Christ's ambassadors and as workplace managers, pastors and church leaders, teachers and coaches, parents and spouses need to perceive ourselves as servant-leaders to those entrusted to our care. The words of our Lord to His disciples ring true as sharply TODAY as they did then, *"He who is greatest among you shall be your servant."* Matthew 23:11. Also after washing His disciples' feet (including His betrayer's feet), Jesus said, *"You call me Teacher and Lord, and you say well, for so I am. If I then, your Lord and Teacher, have washed your feet, you also ought to wash one another's feet. For I have given you an example, that you should do as I have done..."* John 13: 13-17. On another occasion, Jesus told His disciples that He had not come to be served but to serve (Matthew 20: 27-28).

As God told Elijah to anoint Elisha to take his place (1Kings 19:16, 19), similarly, He gave Jesus direction and authority to anoint every believer. As Elijah cast his mantle upon Elisha, so Christ casts the mantle of the Holy Spirit upon every believer. Just as Elisha, who wanted a double portion of Elijah's spirit, was required to keep his eyes on Elijah, likewise we go in the power of the Holy Spirit, and we keep our mind stayed upon the great High Priest, Servant-Leader, who is the Lamb upon the throne! See Hebrews 12: 2. All of us believers are leaders but we are simultaneously called to be a minister to others. **Father's business to serve, however, is not to be mistaken as weakness.** In fact, like God told Joshua, it takes being strong and courageous

– not being afraid. See Joshua 1:9. It requires being **"perfectly weak"** to let God work through us.

What does God look for as the raw material to work Christ – The Servant Leader – into us? The answer is, *"Let this mind be in you which was also in Christ Jesus, who, being in the form of God, did not consider it robbery to be equal with God, but made himself of no reputation, taking the form of a servant, and coming in the likeness of men...He humbled himself and became obedient to the point of death, even the death of the cross. Therefore, God has highly exalted him."* Philippians 2: 5-9. The first raw material is not being anxious to rise to leadership. God leads, we follow. We trust our Father's timing and simply follow Jesus as did Simon of Cyrene, who bore his cross and followed him to Calvary. Secondly, God wants us not to seek any reputation. All the glory goes to Christ. **He made something beautiful about our lives – not us**. The work is not by our power or might, but by His Spirit. Then God looks for the raw material of being able to relate to all men. "There but for the grace of God go I" material. The grain of wheat material (John 12:24) that will be "grounded into flour" to bring the Bread of Life to all men. He looks for the meekness (e.g. being teachable) to be directed for service at the slightest tug of the Master, and the perseverance to endure hardship, while learning to have compassion on all men. And finally, He looks for the raw material of humility to trust Him and to listen. To develop us, He will need to lead us into places we won't want to go – like Peter (John 21:18).

Will we trust in the Lord will all our hearts and lean not on our own understanding? See Proverbs 3:5. Will we believe in Him? Will we believe that *"all things work together for good to those who love God to those who are called according to his purpose"* (Romans 8:28)? The Great Fisher of Men leads us often into deep waters where only Christ's outstretched, nail-driven hands provide the strength to keep serving others. We learn that it was not the nails that held Christ to the cross. Through it all, He presses into us the servant-leader qualities of self-sacrifice, faithfulness, endurance, patience and love.

We are leader-pilgrims in the world, wearing the mantle of the Holy Spirit. Does God's development process to make us **"perfectly weak"** servant-leaders ever end? The answer is that as long as the natural man lives in us we never arrive. Though we surrender to the Lord's correction, and he (e.g. the natural man) is progressively reduced in us so Christ may increase, while we sojourn here we are always the Lord's leadership "trainees." While we serve others here, we are in training for a wonderful assignment He has prepared for us in eternity! See Revelation 5:10 and 22:5.

Chapter 2

The Church – Gates of Hell Shall Not Prevail

Keep Me[3]

In this wicked world am I,
Watch Thou o'er me from on high;
Keep my soul, lest I should be
Led astray, O Lord, from Thee.

Keep me spotless, keep me pure,
Keep me lest the world allure;
Keep me in Thy secret place,
Where I e'er may see Thy face.

Keep me guiltless night and day,
Help me Thy commands obey;
Keep me humble, let not pride
Ever in my soul abide.

Keep me gentle, let no word
From my lips be ever heard
That shall wound a tender heart,
Cause a tear of grief to start.

Refrain:
All I am or hope to be,
I commit, dear Lord, to Thee;
Oh, preserve me in Thy love,
Till I reach Thy courts above.

---

[3] Charles W. Naylor, *pub.*1911

THE CHURCH – HER HEALTH & INFLUENCE

When will the Body of Christ realize that its influence and health is steadily weakened by members hurting one another? Appealing to their flesh, Satan and his "angels of light" ambush sincere Christians who then become like "wolves in sheep's clothing", and hurt other Christians. Instead of making disciples, these "walking wounded" search for what they consider a "real New Testament church" – only to be disillusioned again and again.

The Barna Research Institute reveals that 20% of church-goers change their church every year. 15-20% of them attend more than one church on a rotating basis. Barna says that the American church desperately needs a back-to-basics movement to fill the cracks in our spiritual understanding. And, though pastors say their #1 priority is evangelism, we are still losing the battle for souls in America.

In these devotional messages, we'll see through the wisdom of Scripture and my own experiences how to avoid the enemy's snares, escape entrapment, live and lead in Christ's likeness. So we no longer pass by our wounded brethren ambushed along the Jericho road! We'll disclose the devil's game plan for Christians (Galatians 5:15) and Christ's countermeasures. The devil's devices are foiled by adopting Christ's regular diet of the right habits – called spiritual vitamins; His values and behaviors – called supplements for the soul; and by our realizing the wonder of the Judgment Seat of Christ.

We'll examine a very practical cure for destructive confrontation, along with a template for biblically educating and assimilating church members into the Body of Christ. Some of us have attended church for many years while others are relatively new Christians. Do we all need some re-evangelizing? Do we all need to be re-assimilated into the Church? Why? It's because we may have some very unbiblical understanding about the Church – especially concerning our commitments and responsibilities.

This seems to be the age of deception. Church leaders, who should know better, have their churches acting like cults. Christians, not rooted and grounded in Bible truth, are being deceived. Christians, unaware of how to keep their Christian lives connected to Christ, seem bewildered and unable to cope with things that happen to them and their loved ones. There's persecution for what seems like no reason at all; families being torn apart; splits in churches and (as mentioned earlier) Christians ambushing one another; there's politics for "spiritual profit"; immorality of church leaders; denominational boundaries and distrust of others; and a drift by many away from organized Christianity. Christians want and must have answers, "What's this Christian life really all about? **Why do we have all this deception and these conflicts in our churches?**

Church leaders and members often seem unable or unwilling to deal with sins of the flesh either in other church members or in themselves. These sins give rise to broken relationships among church members and relocation of Christians to other churches (i.e. "shifting saints"). Anger, envy, arrogance, disrespect, slander, and other "crimes" against the brethren go unchecked in our churches. It's no wonder we are losing ground in evangelizing the lost when Jesus, our Lord and Head of the Church, said that unity of Christians was the key to evangelizing the world. In His prayer to our Father in Heaven, He prayed about us, *"...that all of them may be one, Father, just as you are in me and I am in you.* ***May they also be one in us so that the world may believe that you have sent me."*** John 17:21 NIV.

The local church needs to be shaken out of her complacency and tolerance for evil, and awaken to a reality that can (and should) be ours in Christ. Instead of breeding criminals in our midst, (see

Matthew 13: 24-29), who are not confronted for their crimes, we should raise up transformed believers who are effectively educated in what it means to belong to Christ and His Church – believers who are fervent in their commitment and responsibilities to one another – believers who maintain the unity of the Spirit in the bond of peace without compromising their stand for Christ – believers who are keenly aware of the devil's game plan for Christians and our Lord's strategy for near-term as well as ultimate victory over him.

WHAT WE OFTEN DO WITH GOD'S FAITHFULNESS

It's important for Christians to know that whatever befalls us, God is always working things together for good. God is faithful – no matter what. When the enemy comes in like a flood, the Spirit of the Lord will lift up a standard against him (Isaiah 59:19). That doesn't mean that Christians won't have hardships and be ambushed by Satan and his demons. But it does mean that He who is in us is greater than he that is in the world. "In all things, God works for the good of those who love Him, who have been called according to His purpose." (Romans 8:28 NIV)

God is faithful in our trials and temptations. "There has no temptation taken you but such as is common to man: but God is faithful, who will not suffer you to be tempted above that ye are able; but will with the temptation also make a way of escape, that ye may be able to bear it." (1 Corinthians 10:13)

God is faithful in persecutions and difficulties that come from others. "You, however, know all about my teaching, my way of life, my purpose, faith, patience, love, endurance, persecutions, sufferings – what kinds of things happened to me in Antioch, Iconium and Lystra, the persecutions I endured. Yet the Lord rescued me from all of them. In fact, everyone who wants to live a godly life in Christ Jesus will be persecuted." (2Timothy 3:10-12 NIV)

God is faithful in our fear and uncertainty. "He that dwelleth in the secret place of the most High shall abide under the shadow of the Almighty. I will say of the Lord, He is my refuge and my fortress: my God; in him will I trust. Surely he shall deliver thee from the snare of the fowler, and from the noisome pestilence. He shall cover thee with his feathers, and under his wings shalt thou trust: his truth shall be thy shield and buckler. Thou shalt not be afraid…" (Psalm 91:1-5). God uses all our circumstances for our good – to shape us into the image of our Lord and Savior, Jesus Christ.

We Christians, however, shouldn't – because of God's great faithfulness - be tolerating the snares of the devil, and allowing ourselves to hurt, ambush, and entrap one another. That's ridiculous! Young's Compact Dictionary says that an ***ambush*** is a surprise or concealed attack. It usually involves a lure or snare to entrap its victim. A number of things are called snares in Scripture (e.g. riches, false gods, false prophets, and slanderers in Deuteronomy 7:16, Hosea 9:8, and 1Timothy 3:7; 6:9). The child of God is warned against the wiles and snares set by the devil to entrap him (2 Timothy 2:26).

Our Daily Bread, April 3, 1992, gives us this warning: "Many Christians make a…mistake of using their freedom in Christ…they have the idea that they can sin without suffering the consequences. Paul said emphatically, 'Certainly not!' People who think this way may be giving evidence that they have never really chosen God's way – they are still slaves of sin. But even those who are saved, 1 Corinthians 11:32 and Hebrews 12:6 make it clear that God chastens His children when they are disobedient. Yes we are free from the Old Testament rules and regulations. Yes, we are free from the burden of trying to earn our way into heaven. But this freedom does not give us license to sin. It obligates us to a life of grateful obedience."

Yet we in the Church today commit shameful spiritual crimes against one another. We'd do well to hear what our Lord told His people through Hosea. Hosea 6: 8-9 NIV says, "Gilead is a city of wicked men, stained with the footprints of blood. As marauders lie in ambush for a man, so do bands of priests; they murder on the road to Shechem, committing ***shameful crimes***."

Do you know or have you ever been **Evie Envy**? Evie Envy *was a member of the ladies group at her church. Clear Lee Sincere was the leader. Evie Envy was jealous of Clear and had influence with the pastor's wife. She used this influence to get things done the way she wanted in the group. She took away some of the special heart-to-heart ministries that Clear Lee Sincere had instituted and also made the meetings much less nurturing than before. As a result, attendance became more forced than spontaneous. Clear Lee was hurt and suffered in silence through the rest of her term in office. She refused to run for leadership the following year and Evie Envy became the new leader. Eventually the group dwindled and was abandoned.*

Young says that envy is similar to conflict, divisions, and jealousy. Envy is in the depth of man's heart (Mark 7:22). It's a work of the flesh (Galatians 5: 20-21). It's an ingredient of earthly "wisdom." It's "devilish" (James 3:14-15). True love does not envy. (1 Corinthians 13: 4). Whenever we allow ourselves to envy one another, instead of perceiving brothers and sisters in Christ as "friends", we see them as our "competitors." We envy each other over our spouses, children, homes, education, financial security, and material possessions. We even envy one another about our Christian ministries – especially when we see someone getting more visibility and recognition than we from our leaders.

When this happens, we build spiritual walls instead of bridges between us. The flow of encouragement, admonishment, and bearing one another's burdens is hindered. We may allow people to minister to us outwardly, but inwardly we don't receive these brethren as "gifts of God" to us. We inwardly hope they might fail in some way so we can feel better about our own lives and what we possess. When envy occurs between a church leader (e.g. the pastor) and a church member who is gifted in his ministry, both of them become entrapped, discouraged, and less effective.

God is faithful indeed, but sin is serious – even for Christians!

SINNING IS SERIOUS – EVEN FOR CHRISTIANS

Our Lord has given the American Church a second chance under a moral leader, President George W. Bush. The Church (that's us) must stop hiding in fox holes – come out of the closet - and take a stand for the Lord Jesus Christ and His values. We must not be complacent with evil, or our love will grow cold because iniquity will abound more and more in the Church. We must see what's happening in our world. And see how that world is invading the Church. I believe that the Lord is warning His Church to awake out of sleep - discern the signs of the times - and be ready for Him. Luke 12: 34-37.

I believe He is showing us what happens when the Church becomes complacent, divided, and self-involved – rather than being desperate for His Word, maintaining the unity of the Spirit in the bond of peace, and reaching out to the lost. Do you see the worldwide terrorism; the glorification of self and materialism; the blatant attacks on marriage and other godly values; Islamic brutality; militant homosexuality; vileness of TV and movies; the widespread molestation of children; kids killing kids; and, **the infestation of iniquity in the Church**? And all that has been under restraint it seems till now. This is unrestrained lawlessness – no respect for God's law. 2 Thessalonians 2:7. The Church needs to better understand that Christ wants to find F.A.I.T.H when He returns: **F**orsaking **A**ll **I** **T**rust **H**im. Luke 18:8.

There's people in the Church who are like wolves in sheep's clothing who ambush Christians and drive 15% - 20% of them out of their church every year looking for what they consider a real New Testament church – only to be disillusioned again and again. Here are some of the lawless spiritual criminals that do this: Evie Envy, Aaron Arrogance; Angela Angry; Rep Torn; Giddy Gossip;

Dizzy Disrespect; Grey Betray; Pastor Pushy; Rosco Macho; and others. And if they didn't cause enough iniquity on their own, many churches also act like cults by twisting Scripture.

Do you know anyone who's been ambushed by immoral acts? If so, then you've met Rosco Macho. He's the one who romances all the married women in the church. *When I met him, he was a married man with four children. His wife, Faith Full, loved him very much. He was active in the men's group in his church and even taught a class for new believers. Faith Full had a friend named Dis Content, who had a husband and three children of her own. Dis Content had lost a lot of weight since she was married and Rosco Macho found her very attractive. Whenever Dis Content had problems in her family, she would call Rosco Macho to advise her. They spent a lot of time alone and eventually had an affair. Faith Full remained with Rosco Macho in spite of his unfaithfulness but Dis Content left the church and her husband. The kids were split up. Roscoe Macho remained in the church. He had other affairs – once parading his "latest" at a church picnic with Faith Full and his children. Eventually, Faith Full left him and Rosco Macho left the church.*

Sexual sins among Christians entrap believers by causing separation and divorce. Marriages are destroyed. Family members are estranged. Friendships are destroyed because of lust for the wife or husband of another. Sometimes eternal life itself is lost because of the hurt this causes. Christians are caught unaware of their mate's unfaithfulness, and the shock and feeling of betrayal is blamed on the Precious Savior who gave His life for both parties. Christians, who are friends with the estranged couple, are also estranged from one another. In its wake there's a trail of mixed loyalty and love as well as unspoken loss of faith.

The Apostle Paul said, "It is God's will that you should be holy; that you should avoid sexual immorality; that each of you should learn to control his own body in a way that is holy and honorable, not in passionate lust like the heathen, who do not know God; and that in this matter no one should wrong his brother or take advantage of him. The Lord will punish men for all such sins…Therefore, he who rejects this instruction does not reject man but God, who gives you his Holy Spirit." 1 Thessalonians 4:2-8.

A casual attitude toward sin has serious consequences for Christians. Paul says in Galatians 5: 13-14, "You, my brothers, were called to be free. But do not use your freedom to indulge the sinful nature (*or the flesh*); rather, serve one another in love. The entire law is summed up in a single command: "Love your neighbor as yourself."" Paul makes very clear that sinning is serious business. We haven't been saved to sin but to serve one another – showing we love the Lord by loving others, especially those He gives us as brethren.

This is much like Christ's words in John 13: 34-35, "A new commandment I give you: Love one another. As I have loved you, so you must love one another. All men will know that you are my disciples if you love one another." Many Christians say they love the Lord, but how can we measure our love? He said, "If you love me, you will do what I command." John 14:15. "If anyone loves me, he will obey my teaching." John 14:23. In Luke 6:46, before the Lord explains about building the house of our lives on Him (our Rock), He said, "Why do you call me 'Lord, Lord,' and do not what I say?"

Paul goes on to identify the acts of the sinful nature in Galatians 5:19-21. They include the "ambushes" mentioned above (e.g. sexual immorality, impurity, hatred, discord, jealousy, anger, selfish ambition, dissentions, envy, etc.). Then comes a very sobering word for those who engage in these offenses, ***"I warn you, as I did before, that those who live like this will not inherit the kingdom of God."*** Galatians 5:21.

Paul is not condemning Christians who sin. He is condemning those who have no remorse when they sin and continue sinning. <u>Sin should bother us</u>! We must confess our sin and determine not to do it again! 1 John 1:9. The Lord told **<u>us</u>** in Matthew 24: 12,

"Because of the increase of wickedness, the love of most will grow cold, but he who stands firm to the end will be saved." Don't let that be said of you or me – that we begin to act more like the world's wickedness and sin than like Christ and His love for others.

Let's remember the Lord's words about His return in Mark 13:35-37, "So you must keep watch because you do not know when the owner of the house will come back – whether in the evening, or at midnight, or when the rooster crows, or at dawn. If he comes suddenly, don't let him find you sleeping. What I say to you, I say to everyone: 'Watch.'"

Indifference to evil is a great evil!

GOD'S GAME PLAN FOR CHRISTIANS

In previous articles we've discussed how church members and pastors ambush each other; how sinning is serious even for Christians; and how thankfulness can make our hearts more tender toward one another and cause Satan to be ambushed. This article is about God's plan for Christians to avoid destructive confrontation.

If Christians followed the guidance of James 4:6 -10, we wouldn't be ambushing one another. In verse 6 we read, *"...God resists the proud but gives grace to the humble."* We need to humble ourselves and confess our guilt before God. We need to confess our sins and agree with God that we have wronged our brothers and sisters. Our bitterness, lack of forgiveness, envy, betrayal, pride, immorality, slander, anger, and stealing against our brethren in Christ has wronged not only them but disappointed, shamed, and driven nails afresh into our Savior's old wounds! We need to repent over our sins toward the pastor God has given us – our laziness and gossip, our power-plays, lack of respect, submission, and obedience, our unbelief and over-bearing demands. Pastors need to confess their sins against their people – the patronizing, pushing, their insecurity and competitiveness, and their false promises.

We must not only admit our wrongs, but be willing to turn from them and surrender to God's transforming power (Romans 12:1-2). **We must admit that we've enjoyed being "saved" by our Savior but fallen short of truly listening to Him as Lord!** We must daily confess our sins in order to stay close to Him and grow spiritually. He is faithful and just to forgive us when we truly repent and confess our sins (1 John 1:9).

James 4: 7-10 continues, *"Submit yourselves, then, to God. Resist the devil and he will flee from you. Come near to God and he will come near to you. Wash your hands, you sinners, and purify your hearts, you double-minded. Grieve, mourn and wail. Change your laughter to mourning and your joy to gloom. Humble yourselves before the Lord, and he will lift you up."* We allow the devil to ambush us or to use us to ambush others because we don't truly want to OR are ignorant of how to *"submit ourselves and come near to God."* Light dispels darkness. Christians need to embrace the "light" – the knowledge of Christ.

1 John 1:6-7 says, *"If we claim to have fellowship with him yet walk in the darkness, we lie and do not put the truth into practice. But if we walk in the light, as he is in the light, we have fellowship with one another, and the blood of Jesus, his Son, purifies us from every sin."* We need to walk where Jesus walks – in the light with understanding. Then we will have "fellowship" with each other – we will share life the way God intended. We'll accept one another the way we are till God shapes us into what He wants us to be.

We need to stop living by flesh and start living by faith. We need to stop living as "carnal Christians", allowing our natural man and his values to dominate and drive our lives. That's how the devil gets a foothold in our lives and ambushes us and our brothers and sisters in Christ. In addition, when the flesh dominates, the unsaved see "self" in the church instead of seeing Christ – as the Lord intended (John 17:21). Paul put it this way to the Galatians: *"If you keep on biting and devouring each other, watch out or you will be destroyed by each other."* Galatians 5:15. ***The devil's plan is to have Christians destroy one another!*** *"So I say, live by the Spirit, and you will not gratify the desires of the sinful nature. For the sinful nature desires what is contrary to the Spirit, and the Spirit what is contrary to the sinful nature. They are in conflict with each other, so that you do not do what you want."* Galatians 5: 16-17.

Instead of living by flesh, we need to let the Lord power our lives by the Holy Spirit who lives in us. As Jacob, representing the flesh, was wrestled and pinned to the ground by God's Angel, so our flesh must also be pinned. Only then can we be "victors" and become the "Israel" of God. Genesis 32:24-32. When we come to Christ, the "old-man" in us is crucified with Christ (Romans 6:6), and the Holy Spirit enters our lives. But the "natural man" or "the flesh" is also alive and well in us and competes with Christ (i.e. the Holy Spirit). This natural man must be pinned so Christ can become "all in all" in us.

This is a life-long process which only happens as we follow God's plan for our lives…

First, we need to adopt a regular diet of the right habits that keep our lives connected to Christ – to really be intimate with *Him.* I like to call these "spiritual vitamins." Taking them regularly "weakens us perfectly" (Genesis 17:1). We, like Paul, must be able to say, *"What is more, I consider everything a loss compared to the surpassing greatness of knowing Christ Jesus my Lord, for whose sake I have lost all things. I consider them rubbish, that I may gain Christ...I want to know Christ and the power of his resurrection and the fellowship of sharing in his sufferings, becoming like him in his death, and so, somehow, to attain to the resurrection from the dead."* Philippians 3:8-11.

Next, God gave us "supplements for the soul" to help us understand and embrace what it means to build our lives upon Christ (i.e. "fixing our eyes on Jesus…" Hebrews 12:2). I like to call them Christ's "ValuPak." They are Christ's values - His character qualities and priorities. By embracing these values, we get vigor to emulate Christ's behaviors – to walk in His footsteps. All believers and especially church leaders need to follow Christ in this way for arriving at a safe and trusting church environment where Christians follow Christ in responsible relationships with Him and each other.

Finally, we need to keep before us the wonder as well as the awesome reckoning we will experience at the Judgment Seat of

Christ (2 Corinthians 5:10). There we will face our Lord and be judged for our actions here on earth – both good and bad.

These devotional articles deal with each of these areas to ***change the coldness in the church to a love for God, His work, and our brethren; and also to change the iniquity in the church to a seeking first God's kingdom and His righteousness!***

A CALL FOR BELIEVERS TO "GAIN" CHRIST

"...I consider everything a loss compared to the surpassing greatness of knowing Christ Jesus my Lord, for whose sake I have lost all things. I consider them rubbish, that I may gain Christ...I want to know Christ and the power of his resurrection and the fellowship of sharing in his sufferings, becoming like him in death, and so, somehow, to attain to the resurrection from the dead." Philippians 3: 8-10.

In other articles, we've seen ways that church members ambush each other and the pastor, and how pastors ambush church members – how we play into the devil's game plan for Christians to destroy one another. Galatians 5:15. To counter that, God provides us with "spiritual vitamins" – Bible Study, Prayer, Worship, Service, Fellowship, and Comforting Others. He also gives us Christ's priorities and character qualities to embrace (i.e. His values) – Serving Others; Heart-to-Heart; Wisdom From Above; and, Pull-Don't Push. In addition, the Lord gives us a vivid portrait of Christ's judgment of Christians to dwell upon.

To avoid destructive confrontation and recapture for our churches a testimony in our communities – one having the impact on society and culture like the first-century church - we must ask ourselves, **"Do I consider becoming like Christ to be the finish line of my faith – the Prize of running the race of life God's way?"** The state of the Church is in our hands! As we run this race, we need to proactively pursue being people who have a Christ-centered world view with Christ's values and behaviors. We need a new paradigm for living. Hebrews 12:1 advises us to *"...lay aside the weight and the sin that so easily besets, and run with patience the race that is set before us, looking unto Jesus, the Author and Finisher of our faith..."* We need to shed the weight of our egos and materialistic priorities. Instead of serving self, we need to serve Christ and others. We must keep our eyes stayed upon Christ as we patiently and courageously run.

As we draw near to God (James 4:8), we put to death our critical, rebellious, selfish, and sinful ways. Colossians 3:5. The old patterns (i.e. old paradigm) of living cannot survive. The closer we get in our relationship with the Lord the more we leave the world behind. Colossians 3:1 encourages us to seek those things that are above, where Christ is seated at the right hand of God.

The events in the lives of Elijah and Elisha (2 Kings 2) help us to understand what this means and how we are to run the race of life God's way. God was about to take Elijah home and so Elisha asked Elijah for a double portion of his spirit. Elijah told him that in order to have that double portion, the prophet would have to see God take him home. If he did, then Elijah would drop his mantle for Elisha and he would in deed have a double portion of his spirit.

This idea of "watching" is very important to "winning" the Christian race. "Watching" Jesus helps us win "The Prize" of the race. That Prize is Christ – shaped into His image. As we watch and follow Him we become more like Him. In Philippians 3: 13, the Apostle Paul says, *"Not as though I have already attained, but this one thing I do: Forgetting what is past and reaching forth to what is before, I press toward the mark toward the prize of the high calling of God in Christ Jesus."*

Many of us are familiar with Psalm 23: *"The Lord is my shepherd, I shall not want. He maketh me to lie down in green pastures: he leadeth me beside the still waters..."* Do you know that Jesus Christ, Himself, is the "green pastures" and "still waters"? He is the nourishment that energizes us to run the race of life God's way. Jesus said of Himself, *"I am the bread of life: he that cometh to me shall never hunger; and he that believeth on me shall never thirst."* John 6:35. If we do not allow Jesus to satisfy our hunger and thirst, we will starve. There's a thirst that only He can quench. It's like the marathon runners who must consume water to keep pressing ahead. These runners reach out to grab a bottle of water from a stranger along the course because they know it's critical to winning. *"Like the hart (i.e. deer) panteth after the water brooks, so panteth my soul after thee, O God."* Psalm 42:1. Sheep are afraid of a moving stream – running water – so the Lord leads us to "still waters" (i.e. Himself) where His perfect love casts out our fear and we drink freely and abundantly from Him drawing strength to continue running. Often as we run, the Lord beckons us to Himself – to rest a while in green pastures at the still waters – to regain our strength.

Jesus is also "The Finish Line" of our race – to be like Him. Runners "kick" hardest when they are in the final turn and "see" the finish line just ahead! To help us "see" Christ, the Scripture is replete with "portraits of Christ". I think the three best portraits are painted by Paul, Isaiah, and John. I believe that the Gospel of John presents the best portrait because each chapter portrays a different aspect of His character.

Elisha followed Elijah wherever he went and never let him out of his sight. When God sent the fiery chariot to speed Elijah home, Elisha was faithfully watching his master and Elijah dropped his mantle for him. Immediately, Elisha went to see if he had a double portion of Elijah's spirit. He picked up the mantle and went to the Jordan river. He cracked the mantle on the river and said, "Where is the God of Elijah?" The Jordan parted and he walked across on dry ground. He had that double portion of God's Spirit and from then on did many exploits for God.

As Elisha followed Elijah and saw God take him home, and received the double portion of Elijah's spirit, let us "follow" our Lord by taking our spiritual vitamins and embracing His values. Let us enthusiastically take up the mantle of the Holy Spirit that Christ has "dropped" to help us make disciples of all nations. Let us follow Him closely and emulate what we see in Him. The state of the Church is in our hands!

DEVELOPING A HEART IN THE CHURCH FOR SERVING

Our Lord gave every believer the responsibility for making disciples (Matthew 28: 18-20). He said that the greatest in His kingdom was the *servant* of all; and He left us His own example to emulate in developing a heart in those disciples for *serving others*.

In whatever we do as Christians, we are about Father's business – the business of making disciples of all nations. Each of us has a role to play. We don't all have the same function. Some plant seeds while others reap the harvest. Some are apostles – pioneering new works for the Lord. Others are evangelists, who have the gift of witnessing for Him in an especially effective way. Some are missionaries – some with designated positions and others who by their words and behavior are missionaries to wherever they gravitate. Some are pastors – some with designated positions and others who are just influential in another's life. Some are teachers – some with the gift of teaching demonstrated by teaching a bible study, home group, discipleship class, etc. - others teach by example and by their testimonies.

There are many other areas of ministry and the Church matures as we "touch" one another's lives with these ministries (Ephesians 4:16). As we disciple others and help them determine Father's calling on their lives for His business, we need to help them *identify their specific products and services*. For some the service may be administration and the product might be an organized ministry team. To another, the service might be helping and the product might be a less-pressured husband or wife more prepared to serve the Lord.

Jesus had both products and services. His products are transformed people – like you and me. His services are many. They include: salvation; maintaining our lives by His Lordship; setting us in a local church to serve one another (i.e. our internal customers); empowering us to reach the unsaved (i.e. our external customers); developing a heart in us for obeying our heavenly Father.

The people we serve become our "customers" in Father's business. So to get a heart in our people for serving others, we also need to ask them, *"Who are your customers? Who are you serving? What are their names?"* We serve God first – that is always true. God then invites us to join Him in serving others. Jesus' primary customer was His heavenly Father. He was always about Father's business (Luke 2:49). His Father rated Christ's performance, *"This is my beloved Son, in whom I am well pleased..."* (Matthew 17:5). Also Jesus needed to show Himself to His Father after the resurrection. *"Jesus saith unto her, Touch me not; for I am not yet ascended to my Father..."* (John 20:17) Christ's secondary customers, of course, were all of us – the sick (i.e. sinners) who needed a Physician to save them.

We also need to equip our people for serving these customers effectively. They need *the experience and example of mature believers* in their ministry. They need as much *information, knowledge, and ministry resources* as are available. They need to know *the basics from you (their mentor) of Bible study, prayer, worship, and fellowship*. Our objective as disciple-makers is to give them competence and confidence in serving others. In addition, we need to *teach them to manage "moments of truth" well.* These moments are when their customers will be watching them ever so much closer than normal and evaluating their performance.

Every job has moments when customers evaluate the service they are receiving. In restaurants, we subconsciously rate service by such things as ambiance or the greeting of the hostess, or how our menus are presented to us, or whether our meal has the same size portion as the person with whom we're eating. Jesus had many moments of truth. One example was when the Pharisees tried to entangle Him in His talk. They sent the Herodians to ask Him, *"Is it lawful to give tribute unto Caesar or not?"* The Father and His disciples must have been listening very closely for Christ's answer. *"Render therefore unto Caesar the things that are Caesar's and unto God the things that are God's."* (Matthew 22:21). There were many other "moments" that Jesus managed well, pleasing the One He served. We must teach our people to effectively manage their moments of truth as well.

Besides working with our people to decide what their products and services are; who their customers are; equipping them to serve competently and confidently; and, teaching them to manage moments of truth, we also need to *help them determine how to measure success*. Though quantities are often used to determine how successful we are in making disciples, it's really the quality of those disciples that matters most. Quality disciples make other quality disciples – *"By this shall all men know that you are my disciples, if you have love one to another."* (John 13:35)

As an illustration, suppose you're working to develop a heart for serving in a Sunday School teacher. Here's what you might conclude are his/her products, services, customers, equipping resources, measurement criteria, and moments of truth: A teacher's products are transformed lives – making students become more like Christ - to keep students focused upon Christ and the finish line (Hebrews 12:1-2; Philippians 3:10-14). A teacher's services are as varied as it takes to make disciples – whatever's needed (Romans 12:1-2). A teacher's primary customer is Christ. He is the One *who "gave some apostles; and some prophets; and some evangelists; and some pastors and teachers..."* (Ephesians 4:11) Their secondary customers include other believers and maybe unbelievers in their class.

Teachers must be equipped for service by regularly studying the Word, and through prayer, worship, and fellowship with other believers. We also equip teachers by showing them how to deal with the "storms of life." We measure a teacher's success by the standard of Galatians 5:22-26, the fruit of the Spirit. We measure the degree of cooperation and camaraderie among their students. We also measure the teacher's faithfulness in serving his/her students (Luke 12:35). A survey of students may help us.

Teachers must always remember Isaiah 55:10-11, especially when results are difficult to "see". *"For as the rain cometh down, and the snow from heaven, and returneth not thither, but watereth the earth, and maketh it bring forth and bud, that it may give seed to the sower, bread to the eater: So shall my word be that goeth forth out of my mouth: it shall not return unto me void, but it shall accomplish that which I please, and it shall prosper in the thing whereto I sent it."* Finally, an important "moment of truth" for a teacher is speaking the truth in love even when it is unpopular.

REMEMBER TO BE THANKFUL

Thanking and praising our Father brings a peace to our souls like nothing else can. And that peace is then extended to members of His family. But we can't be at peace with Him if we are at war with His children – our brothers and sisters. This "war" cuts us off from the support and enjoyment we need that He has provided through His other children. It also plays into the devil's plans to cause Christians to destroy one another. See Galatians 5: 15.

Ensnare the devil – not one another. Stay in a continual attitude of gratitude knowing that the Lord *"works for the good of those who love Him, who have been called according to His purpose."* See Romans 8: 28. The devil's deceit and trickery is foiled when we thank God throughout our circumstances. God will turn the tables and ambush him. See 2 Chronicles 20. There are many reasons for thanking God. Here are some to keep in mind when the going gets tough! Just remember, "WE MUST ALWAYS THANK CHRIST".

WE

W – *Worship.* When we worship Him, our whole countenance seems to smile.
E - *Eternal Life.* When we're there ten thousand years, bright shining as the sun, we've no less days to give God praise than when we first begun! See Daniel 12:3

MUST

M – *Miracles.* He does so many that we never see! He heals us and intervenes in our lives to help us get through our circumstances. See Matthew 10: 29-31.

U – *Unity with other believers.* He prayed in John 17:21 that as He was in the Father and the Father in Him, we would be one in the Father and Son, so the world would believe the Father sent Him!
S – *Sacrifice.* We should thank Him for His sacrifice on the cross for us. We should also thank Him because He taught us to sacrifice ourselves for others. He said that the greatest in His kingdom would be the servant of all! See Mark 9: 35.
T – *Teaching.* He's taught us so much from His Word and even given us the Great Commission to teach others. See Matthew 28: 19-20.

ALWAYS

A – *Activity.* We are given so much to do. We are mostly all so active in our homes, our churches, our workplaces, and in our volunteering.
L – *Life More Abundant.* The Christian life is not an easy life; but it is the abundant life when we follow the Good Shepherd. See John 10: 10.
W – *Winner.* We are more than conquerors in every circumstance of life because of His love for us. And we know that He is working everything for good to those who love Him and are called according to His purposes. See Romans 8: 28, 37.
A – *Ambassador.* How great a position He has bestowed upon us to be *"ambassadors for Christ."* See 2 Corinthians 5: 20.
Y – *You & Your Life.* We are still here. And God accepts us as we are, while He shapes us into what He wants us to be! See Romans 12: 1-2 and Philippians 2: 5-12.
S – *Salvation.* Christ's death paid the price God demanded for our sin (i.e. death). God as Judge had sentenced us to death because of our sin. Then God, the Son, came down from His Judgment Seat and took the punishment He had ordered for us! All we needed to do was repent and receive this great gift! See John 3: 16.

THANK

T – *Trials & Suffering.* Through our hardships, Christ is molding us into His own image. In addition, He comforts us in them so we can comfort others with the comfort we've received from Him. See 2 Corinthians 1: 4.
H – *Happiness.* He's given us the secrets to happiness. See Matthew 5: 3-10.
A – *Answers to Prayer.* He said, "Ask and it shall be given; Seek and you shall find; Knock and the door shall be opened to you." See Matthew 7: 7.
N – *New Mercies Every Day.* As we are growing in our relationship with Him, we find new reasons for thanking and praising Him. See Lamentations 3: 23.
K – *Keeping Power.* We should thank Him for His power to keep us on track – also for His love and power to get us back on track when we sin. When we confess our sins, He is faithful and just to forgive us our sin, and to cleanse us from all unrighteousness. See 1 John 1:9.

CHRIST

C – *Comfort.* Trials are tough but His comfort is wonderful! See Isaiah 28: 29.
H – *His Other Children.* Many of us are cut off from physical family members. But the Lord has given us a spiritual family of brothers and sisters who provide us support and enjoyment we need. See Ephesians 4: 13-16.
R – *Righteousness.* He who knew no sin became sin for us so that we might become the righteousness of God in Him! See 2 Corinthians 5: 21.
I – *Invitations.* Jesus is always inviting us to draw closer to Him – He is meek and lowly of heart and will give us rest for our souls. He is also inviting us to walk with Him along the "Gospel Way" in sharing our faith. See Matthew 11: 28.
S – *Service.* Doing God's will and completing the work He's given each of us to do, is the great fulfillment of this life. See John 4: 34.
T – *Timing.* The Lord's timing in our lives is always "on time". He makes all things beautiful in His time! See Ecclesiastes 3: 11.

We, the Church, should remember also to thank God for revealing Himself to us through Jesus Christ. Every chapter of the Gospel of John provides a different attribute of Christ for which to thank God! See if you can find them. And remember to always be thankful!

CHRIST'S JUDGMENT OF HIS CHURCH

The Book of Revelation was written to the seven churches which were representative of all God's people. Jesus told John, *"What thou seest write in a book and send it unto the seven churches which are in Asia..."* Revelation 1:11. As the Righteous Judge of Revelation, Jesus will preside at the White Throne judgment of unbelievers. Revelation 20:11-15. He is also the Judge of believers at the Judgment Seat of Christ. 2 Corinthians 5:10. In Revelation 2 and 3, we see Christ, as Revealer and Righteous Judge demonstrating His grace and the sternness of His love. He's warning us all – through these seven churches - to get ready for His return and His judgment of us.

Before His crucifixion, Jesus prayed to His Father about <u>all</u> His disciples (i.e. the Church), *"That they all may be one; as thou, Father, art in me, and I in thee, that they also may be one in us: that the world may believe that thou hast sent me."* John 17:21. It is eternally important that all Christians - the Body of Christ – the Church – the kingdom of God - maintain the unity of the Spirit in the bond of peace. Ephesians 4: 3. Because by reflecting the image of Christ to the whole watching world, people will believe that God sent Christ - and accept Him.

Because it is so important that the Church emulate Christ, the Revealer and Righteous Judge provided feedback to the seven churches (Revelation 2 and 3) to expose their sin, lead them to repent, and help them mature in His ways and purposes. These churches, though physically in the area now known as Turkey, were not only to be representative of all churches but also representative of us individual Christians and the issues we face. His judgments were for both the Church and individual believers.

To fully understand this, remember the "two kingdoms of God" – a visible and invisible one. The kingdom of God is the spiritual rule of God in the hearts of His people through Jesus Christ. The visible one is called the Church, made up of all those who accept Jesus as Savior and follow Him as Lord. The invisible one is the one within each believer. In Luke 17: 20-21 Jesus said, *"The kingdom of God is within you."* Romans 14:17 says that the kingdom of God *"is righteousness, peace, and joy in the Holy Ghost."* God is working in each of those kingdoms. The visible kingdom, however, only grows as the invisible one in each believer grows and produces the fruit of the Spirit (Galatians 5: 22-26) and the character of Christ (Philippians 2: 5-11).

Ephesus had started out as a "Mary" church – one that sat at the feet of Jesus, her First Love. But the church had become a "Martha" church, whose first love was working in its own strength rather than in the power of the Holy Spirit. **Smyrna** thought it was poor because it didn't have many material possessions – but it was really rich with the gold that comes from having their faith tried in the fire of affliction. 1 Peter 1:7. **Pergamum** was heretical allowing doctrines of devils. Jesus said that He knew where Satan's seat was there. **Thyatira** was tolerating a lying prophetess. Not only were they stretching the truth but they also had serious moral and spiritual compromise. **Sardis** had a better reputation than they deserved because they were dying spiritually. **Philadelphia** was a loyal church, which had been obedient to God's Word and developed Christ's character. **Laodicea** was lukewarm and self-satisfied, which form the foundation for rebellion and falling away.

These same attitudes and behaviors are in the Church today. And, regrettably, they remain *in us* who call ourselves Christians. Our Precious Lord in His grace is warning (and challenging) churches in His visible kingdom, and we individuals in the invisible kingdom. He's giving us time to better prepare for His return – to live NOW with a view toward ETERNITY. Here are the main messages to the seven churches:

1. Before each judgment, the Lord always presented a portrait of Himself that the particular church needed to see. For example, to the Philadelphia church He introduced Himself as, *"...he that is holy, he that is true, he that hath the key of David, he that openeth and no man shutteth; and shutteth and no man openeth..."* He was telling them (and us) to always keep a picture of Him (i.e. who He is) in the center of their (and our) hearts and minds.

In Revelation 1, Christ reveals Himself with all the attributes of His character. In Revelation 2 and 3, He then divides up and presents to each of the seven churches the attributes they need. John prayed that these churches would have peace. Revelation 1:4. Jesus then gave them the portrait of Himself that would bring peace. *"Thou will keep him in perfect peace, whose mind is stayed on thee: because he trusteth in thee."* Isaiah 26:3.

2. He told every church that He knew their works. This can be reassuring. But for some of us it should, at times, be disconcerting too! The Lord knows us inside and out. He knows when we hurt one another – how we ambush each other with anger, jealousy, deceit, immorality, slander, lack of forgiveness, pride, stealing, and betrayal.

3. He told four of the seven churches to repent. *"If we confess our sins, he is faithful and just to forgive us our sins, and to cleanse us from all unrighteousness."* 1 John 1:9. We must change the wrong beliefs, attitudes, and behaviors we see in ourselves. We must also take our stand against such things in the Church.

4. He told all the churches to overcome. It's like His message to Joshua as he took charge of God's people, *"There shall not any man be able to stand before thee all the days of thy life: as I was with Moses, so I will be with thee; I will not fail thee, nor forsake*

thee....Only be thou strong and courageous...Be strong and of good courage; be not afraid, neither be thou dismayed: for the Lord thy God is with thee whithersoever thou goest." Joshua 1: 5-9.

Jesus told His disciples, *"Never will I leave you; never will I forsake you."* Hebrews 13:5. We must remember Philippians 4:13, *"I can do everything through him (Christ) who gives me strength."* With the Holy Spirit within to empower each believer, we can in deed overcome - and by unity with our brothers and sisters in Christ, witness to a dying world that Jesus Christ is the only Way to eternal life.

WARM UP! BECOME HEART-TO-HEART

The Lord showed me how we can use the prophet's mantle to learn about how we should treat one another – especially how leaders should treat their people. The mantle (or cloak as it is sometimes translated) was worn by all prophets. It was the "badge" of the prophet – the symbol of his office. It was made of the skins of animals with the hair left on it. Elisha followed Elijah closely before God took him to heaven in a fiery chariot. And Elijah dropped his mantle for Elisha so he could have a double portion of his spirit. See 2 Kings 2: 9-13.

Today's leaders at the workplace, home, church, and school must be a covering, protector, comforter and instrument of empowerment. They must serve and provide freedom, identification and recognition for their people to help them through the uncertainty, change, broken trust and chaos they experience in the world. We Christians need to be examples of what we want our people to become, with them watching us closely, so the mantle (or power to overcome) will fall on them.

As the mantle provided warmth for the prophet, likewise leaders at all levels and in various enterprises (including the church) need to give their people the "warmth" of knowing that they are their leader's highest concern and most precious asset. As the mantle felt the prophet's heartbeat, leaders in the home, workplace, church, and classroom need to feel their people's heart beat – their needs, desires, strengths and weaknesses - their goals and life's roadmap. And we need to share ours with them. In short, we need to be Heart – to-Heart like Jesus! It's the only way we'll know how to take them from being "directed" to being "empowered". Needless to say, husbands, wives, and children need to make time to communicate with each other. Pastors and teachers need to get to know their congregations and students if they expect to reach inside with their message.

Jesus put it this way, *"I am the good shepherd; and I know My sheep and am known by My own."* John 10: 14. Speaking of the good shepherd, Jesus said, *"To him the doorkeeper opens; and the sheep hear his voice; and he calls his own sheep by name and he leads them out."* John 10: 3. Man was created to fellowship with God; but that fellowship was broken when Adam and Eve sinned. God wanted that fellowship restored so he came "in the flesh", as Jesus Christ, to die in our place and show us what He was really like. He came so we could get our arms around God and hug the One who loves us most of all.

Jesus said, *"He who has seen Me has seen the Father."* John 14: 9. He also showed us that He cared enough to suffer our temptations. The scripture says, *"For we do not have a High Priest who cannot sympathize with our weaknesses, but was in all points tempted as we are, yet without sin."* Hebrews 4: 15. Jesus knows what it's like to be you and me. He cares enough to have even the hairs on our heads numbered. Matthew 10: 30.

The commitment Jesus wants from us is not to follow all the rules or the whole law out of obligation. That would put us in bondage to fulfill every point of the law. Instead, Jesus paid the price for our breaking the law when He died on the cross and suffered the pains of hell – since death and eternal separation from God was the penalty for breaking the law. He became human to pay our debt, and now we are free to serve Him from our hearts, motivated by love and not fear. Jesus said, *"If you love Me, keep My commandments (from the heart)."* John 14: 15. *"If anyone loves Me, he will keep My word."* John 14: 23. In a similar way, managers, pastors, parents, spouses and teachers must understand that we are dealing with human beings with feelings, concerns and hopes for the future. We need to get a heart commitment from them to gain their full productivity potential – and we need to be sensitive to those things that will reach the heart of people.

Concern for people's needs and knowing them – even to the intentions of the heart – is a cornerstone of Jesus' leadership!

Jesus always took time to get to know people and to meet their needs. Remember blind Bartemaeus. Jesus was headed for Jerusalem. And when Bartemaeus heard that it was Jesus of Nazereth who was passing by, he called out to Him, *"Jesus, thou son of David, have mercy on me."* Luke 18: 38. His disciples told the old man to keep still and not bother the Master. But Jesus wanted to know this man's heart. He said, *"What wilt thou that I do unto thee?"* Zacchaeus was another who wanted to get to know Jesus – and he wasn't disappointed. Jesus looked up into the tree, where this corrupt tax collector had positioned himself to catch a glimpse of the Master, and said, "*Zacchaeus, make haste, and come down; for today I must abide at your house."* Luke 19: 5

See how the Apostle Paul learned both the principles of being a "servant leader" and being "Heart-to-Heart" as he describes his approach to bringing the salvation message to many types of people: *"For though I am free from all men, I have made myself a servant to all, that I might win the more; and to the Jews I became a Jew, that I might win Jews; to those who are under the law, as under the law; to those who are without law, as without law (not being without law toward God, but under law toward Christ), that I might win those who are without law; to the weak I became weak, that I might win the weak. I have become all things to all men, that I might by all means save some."* 1 Corinthians 9: 19-22.

Let's cloth ourselves in Christ's mantle – emulate Him – especially in being Heart-to-Heart with the people He's given us.

LET'S WISE UP!

Last time, we discussed how the Church needs to "warm up" by becoming "Heart-to-Heart" in our relationships with each other. Besides warming up, the Church needs to wise up! James 3:17 says that, *"The wisdom that is from above is first pure, then peaceable, gentle, willing to yield, full of mercy and good fruits (some translations say goodness, fairness, genuineness), without partiality, and without hypocrisy."* Like Jesus, we need to value these qualities – primarily being pure. We need to have pure motives and be people that can be trusted by others to help them through the "storms" of their lives. This is true even in our work life. Many surveys of employees have been done to determine what kind of supervisor they want. The most important quality they want is integrity – someone they can trust.

Elijah's mantle can help us understand the importance of having pure motives and integrity. The mantle was a sleeveless garment made of the skins of animals with the hair left on it. It needed to be thick enough to resist the wind and sand during the storms in the prophet's life. It also couldn't have any tears or holes in it that would let the rain in. In short, it needed to have integrity to protect the prophet from the elements. And if we want to help others through the "storms" of their life – to have them share with us their troubles and seek the insights God gives us – then we must also have pure motives and this wisdom from above.

But how can we measure our "purity" or integrity? It may be a difficult task, but it's extremely important as we *"press on toward the goal to win the prize (i.e. Christ) for which God has called (us) heavenward in Christ Jesus."* Philippians 3: 14. If we, like the Apostle Paul, want to surrender our bodies as living sacrifices for the Lord to transform into the image of Christ, we must examine our hearts – to look for this wisdom which is first pure. The best way I've ever found to do that is to let our Lord Jesus Christ take us on an incredible journey through our hearts. Consider what our Lord might say as He enters each room there. The following is adapted from **My Heart, Christ's Home**, by Robert Boyd Munger, 1986:

In John 14:23, Jesus said, *"If a man loves me he will keep my words: and my Father will love him, and we will come and make our abode with him."* The word "abode" in this verse, is the same word Jesus used when He spoke about preparing a "place" (i.e. abode) for us in heaven. John 14: 3. So while Jesus is preparing a place for us in heaven, we are to prepare a place for Him in our hearts. To determine how we're doing, let's briefly walk through the "rooms" of our heart with Jesus.

THE STUDY (LIBRARY) ROOM – What would Jesus see in your mind? What are the images stored there – the magazines and books we read or the TV programs and movies we watch? Would you be comfortable with Jesus looking at those images? Would He find His picture in the center of that room and the books of the Scriptures on all the book shelves? That's what He wants to see there!
THE DINING ROOM - What would you serve Jesus? What are your appetites and desires? Would you serve Him your education, wealth, family, investments, awards, etc.? If so, Jesus would not eat much and would say, *"I have meat that you know not of – to do the will of my Father who sent me and to finish His work."* John 4: 34.
THE LIVING ROOM – This is the room where Jesus waits to meet us and fellowship with us everyday. Do you read the Word and pray to Him daily? He would tell you that this time is not just for us but also for Him. He paid a great price for us – and delights meeting and fellowshipping with us often. Even when we forget, Jesus is always there in the living room waiting for us!
THE RECREATION ROOM - This is our place of fun and fellowship. Would the Lord find us taking Him with us when we

go out with friends – or would we have to tell Him to wait home because He would feel uncomfortable? He would remind us that we promised to let Him be our Friend and go with us everywhere.

THE WORK ROOM – The Lord would look to see what work we've done for Him lately. We might say that we felt awkward and clumsy in spiritual things and haven't produced much. He would agree and tell us to put ourselves in the control of the Holy Spirit and let Him lead us in doing God's work.

THE BEDROOM – Here the Lord would remind us that He doesn't restrict sex to a marriage relationship because sex is bad but because it is good under the right conditions. When not in marriage, sex can be harmful and destructive.

THE HALL CLOSET – As we are showing the Lord around our heart, He may pass the hall closet and mention that there's a horrible odor coming from there – maybe a few things left over from our old lives – before we asked Him in. He'd want us to clean it. We might tell Him that we didn't have the strength – that these very personal things were too hard for us to let go – that after showing Him all the other rooms, He shouldn't bother us about a 2'x 4' closet! But as we sense Him withdrawing, we'd finally ask Him if He would clean the closet for us. Jesus would say that He'd been waiting a long time for us to ask. Very soon the closet would be clean.

After struggling, trying to keep all the rooms of our heart pure, many of us would then ask the Lord, Himself, to clean our whole house like He did the hall closet. He would say, however, "I can't clean your house because you've only made me a guest here. I don't own the house. First, you must sign the deed of your house over to Me and make Me the owner!" So finally we really do make Him Lord and Master of our heart and lives – and we learn the wisdom that is first pure!

So wise up Church and learn to appreciate and embrace this wisdom from above. It's the holiness of the cross: *"God made him who had no sin to be sin for us, so that in him we might become the righteousness of God."* 2 Corinthians 5: 21.

OPEN HEART SURGERY AND THE CHURCH

If you want to find out how blessed you are as a Christian, try having open heart surgery. That's what happened to me. I had a heart murmur that had gotten a lot louder. An echocardiogram showed I was in trouble. The emergency room doctor at Southern Ocean County Hospital told me they couldn't help me and had me transported by ambulance to Deborah Heart and Lung Center. The next day I went for a catherization. The good news was that there were no blockages in any arteries going to the heart. The valve, however, was pushing a lot of blood back into the heart rather than out to the body. Surgery was scheduled in a few days.

While I waited for surgery, the Lord arranged for various people to share their testimony of God's faithfulness with me – the nurses, nurses' assistants, those who made up the beds, and many more. Phone calls came in from everywhere – besides those from my own church, my former pastor called from Florida – who had the same operation 10 years ago. Another pastor-friend called to tell me his father had the operation. A pastor and her husband prayed together with me on the phone. There were prayers being said for me in Honduras by a medical missionary team there; in Washington State by people who had led me to the Lord 34 years ago; in Nigeria, Africa; on Long Island; in north and south Jersey. It reminded me of how we in the church need to share our testimonies with those searching to find what life is all about by living lives that honor Christ and by faithfully witnessing. We need to assure them that they can place their trust in Christ.

Then came the surgery. There was nothing to do but surrender to the skill and knowledge of the capable doctors. It reminded me of how we must regularly surrender our bodies as living sacrifices (Romans 12: 1-2) to the Lord – how we need to trust in the Lord with all our hearts and lean not on our own understanding (Proverbs 3: 5-6). It also reminded me of the person who finally surrenders to the convicting work of the Holy Spirit (i.e. the "operation" of the Holy Spirit) and receives Christ as Savior and Lord.

After surgery, I went to the Surgical Intensive Care Unit (SICU). It was amazing. Nurses were assigned to me full time 24hours a day. I was her total responsibility while I was there – which turned out to be 2 days. They made me feel so secure in their loving care. Besides all the technical things, she even asked me how I wanted to sleep, and moved me onto my side, bolstering me with pillows and blankets so I would stay in that position. When she thought I was becoming frazzled by watching all the other patients in the SICU, she brought a TV/VCR in and had me choose a movie to watch! We shared The Daily Bread with one nurse. I awoke on the second day in the SICU to a nurse singing, "His eye is on the sparrow and I know He watches me." It made me think that we in the church need to provide one-on-one (heart-to-heart) care for those who come to Christ till they understand what's happened to them and begin feeling secure in the church.

When I was ready, they moved me to a regular room – in the same area where I had been waiting for surgery. The nurses and technicians made me feel so welcomed – like a returning hero! Then came all the testing – echocardiograms, chest x-rays, blood tests, blood pressure, heart rate, temperature, and weight in the wee hours of the morning. It became clear to me that the staff was short-handed – especially when members of the staff called in sick. But that didn't stop the care. Everyone was cross-trained in each others' jobs. So a nurses' assistant might make the bed or serve breakfast, take your vital signs in the early hours, or wheel you to get an x-ray – even though it wasn't her job – so that all the patients could get well. It reminded me of the attitude the early Christians had about caring for each others' needs – so selfless. See Acts 2: 42-47. Christ's Great Commission to make and care for disciples was truly the central motivation of their lives. As a result, the Lord added to their number daily (verse 47), and there was no lack in the Body of Christ.

We'd do well to look at the Church as a hospital for those with broken hearts, and to emulate hospitals like Deborah. Our Great Physician is the head doctor, with each of us as His assistant. The Holy Spirit is the head teacher – building us into a team of people whose aim is to live a life pleasing to the Lord which centers on heart-to-heart caring for others.

Thanks for your many prayers, phone calls, and cards. I never realized how blessed I am! *"...my God shall supply all your need according to His riches in glory by Christ Jesus. Now unto God be glory forever and ever. Amen."* Philippians 4:19-20.

CO-LABORERS IN CHRIST – ENCOURAGE EACH OTHER

One of my favorite memories is leading a group of 150 people and 25 supervisors for 10 years at a place called Picatinny Arsenal in Dover, NJ. Everyone worked as a team in each of six major areas of responsibility to customers. I believe that our success in winning many customer service awards was using a people-management style the Lord gave me based upon Christ's values (i.e. His priorities and character qualities) and the principles of God's Word.

It was so effective that the whole Center (about 4000 people) adopted this management philosophy and began winning awards from POTUS (that's the US President), NJ Governor, the Secretary of Defense, and many others. The Church would do well to adopt the same leadership style.

I called one of Christ's values, "Pull-Don't Push." An important principle that flows from embracing this value is contained in

Hebrews 3: 13, *"...encourage one another daily, as long as it is called Today..."* It's all about building people up rather than dragging them down – about encouraging and empowering them. You can see how it works by considering 1 Kings 19, the story of Elijah and Jezebel.

That evil woman Jezebel wanted to kill Elijah, who, with God's great power, had just defeated the prophets of Baal. Instead of Elijah maintaining faith that God could defeat her too, he ran from her. What would God do to Elijah for his lack of faith? God sent angels to him to feed and strengthen His exhausted prophet. When Elijah found himself in a cave, the word of the Lord came to him, *"What doest thou here, Elijah?"* God listened to his complaints and self-pity and tried to encourage him. Elijah hid his face in his mantle, ashamed of his performance (1Kings 19:13). We shouldn't overpower people into admitting mistakes – we offer a listening and learning opportunity to them so they can get their confidence back. God's primary interest was to get Elijah back to being productive for Him. God needed him to anoint Jehu to be king of Israel and Hazael to be king over Syria. He also needed him to anoint Elisha to be His prophet in Elijah's place.

The key message we need to send to our people is, "I believe in you." I believe you can do the work you are called to do. We can't say that, however, unless we've "empowered" them to do the job – adequately prepared them. This requires that we stay on the "empowerment track" - GIVE DIRECTIONS, COACH, ENCOURAGE, and then EMPOWER. Jesus did this in Luke 10 when He sent His disciples two-by-two into many cities. Jesus gave them directions. He had already coached them on how to do what He required – He was their example. He had allowed the disciples to speak for Him and cast out evil spirits. He had corrected their behavior and encouraged them until they themselves were confident. Then He trusted (i.e. empowered) them to go out without Him.

When they make mistakes, most people already know it. They don't need to be reminded of that. Mainly they need a listening ear and a gentle but firm arm to lean on to help them learn from the experience and get them back on track. The secret is to cast out fear. *"There is no fear in love; but perfect love casteth out fear: because fear hath torment. He that feareth is not made perfect in love."* (1John 4:18) This is what happened with Peter. After he denied the Lord three times, when Jesus met him at the Sea of Galilee, He knew that Peter was sorry for what he had done. Instead of rebuking him and reminding him of his "shortcoming", Jesus encouraged him to be productive in the kingdom. He first asked if Peter loved Him with a love that was selfless, desiring nothing in return (i.e. "agape" love). In addition, Jesus said, *"Do you love me more than these (i.e. other disciples love me)?"* Peter couldn't say he had a completely unselfish love or that he loved Him more than the other disciples. Peter said that he loved the Lord just like a brother would love another brother (i.e. "phileo" love). Jesus said, *"Feed my lambs."* Jesus asked him again if he had an unselfish love. Peter answered it the same way. Jesus said, *"Feed my sheep."* Finally, Jesus asked Peter if he really loved Him like a brother. Peter said that he did, and Jesus said, *"Feed my sheep."* (John 21:15-19) Christ's primary interest was to get Peter back to being productive for Him.

Remember the "bruised reed" of Isaiah's prophecy about Christ, *"A bruised reed shall he not break, and the smoking flax shall he not quench..."* Isaiah 42:3. Shepherds used reeds to play music as they tended their sheep. But after a while the mouthpiece would get wet and soft and be of no use. So the shepherd would throw this "bruised reed" away. When finding it, Jesus wouldn't break it like other shepherds. He would restore it and play beautiful music through it again. Many people we meet and shepherd will feel like bruised reeds. Jesus doesn't break bruised reeds – neither should we! Encourage and empower them!

KINGDOM "KIDS"

In the Kingdom of God, believing on the Son is the greatest challenge. *"Then they asked him (i.e. Jesus), 'What must we do to do the work of God?' Jesus answered, 'The work of God is this: to believe in the one whom he has sent.'"* John 6: 28-29.

Service is the greatest calling. *"When he (i.e. Jesus) had finished washing their feet, he ...returned to his place. 'Do you understand what I have done for you?' he asked them. 'You call me Teacher and Lord, and rightly so, for that is what I am. Now that I your Lord and Teacher, have washed your feet, you also ought to wash one another's feet. I have set an example that you should do as I have done for you.'"* John 13: 13-15.

Jesus also said that the greatest in His kingdom were those who served. Matthew 23:11. Paul, who followed Jesus into many trials and sufferings, told us *"by love serve one another."* Galatians 5:13.

Trusting Christ while serving others is what brings our greatest fulfillment. Jesus said, *"If you know these things, happy are you if you do them."* John 13:17.

Whom do you think Jesus says does these things best in the Kingdom?

In John 1: 12-13, John says that those who receive Christ receive authority to become children of God. *"Yet to all who received him (i.e. Jesus), to those who believed in his name, he gave the right to become children of God – children born not of natural descent, nor of human decision or a husband's will, but born of God."*

Jesus had some strong feelings about these Kingdom "kids." In Mark 10: 13-16, Jesus was very displeased at His disciples for preventing young children from coming to Him. *"When Jesus saw this, he was indignant. He said to them, 'Let the little children come to me, and do not hinder them, for the kingdom of God belongs to such as these.'"* Jesus also told us that unless we receive the Kingdom of God as a young child, we could not enter in. He said, *"I tell you the truth, anyone who will not receive the kingdom of God like a little child will not enter it."* Luke 18: 17.

So what does Jesus mean when He says "as a young child" we must enter His Kingdom? I think He means we must have absolute "trust" or "dependence" upon Him (i.e. believe on Him). He means also that like little children we will always be discovering, reaching out in His Kingdom to try new things – like kids who might put things in their mouths to see what it's all about, always being creative and learning.

I think coming to Him as a young child implies losing our lives as we know them. We need to lose our self sufficiency and independence. Kids know they need others! They're dependent upon their parents. They feel secure in their mother's arms. They sense a need to play with other kids! Jesus said that if we love our life, we'll lose it, but if we lose our lives by depending upon Him, serving Him – and others through Him -we'll keep it for eternity. John 12:25. He goes on in Matthew 16: 24 to say that if we want to follow Him, we must deny self, take up our cross, and follow Him.

Remember, Jesus came to us as a child! So it is perfectly reasonable that we should come to Him that way also. *"Do not conform any longer to the pattern of this world, but be transformed by the renewing of your mind. Then you will be able to test and approve what God's will is – his good, pleasing and perfect will."* Romans 12:2.

So then, when we receive Jesus, He gives us power (or the right) to be a child (and by the way an heir to the Kingdom) and follow

Christ on the journey to being shaped into His image. Philippians 3: 12-14. This process of following Jesus is actually the goal – for if we follow Him, we'll become like Him. What man considers a process, God considers the goal.

Believing on Christ is doing the work of God (i.e. trusting and following Him every day in every way). When we do follow Him, He leads us into self-sacrificing service and love to others. He leads us to the greatest fulfillment man can know – doing the will of God and completing the work He's given us to do. John 4: 34.

When we find the child-like, God-dependent life, we are then free from our fears and insecurities that bind us to a flesh-life; and without hidden agendas, we surrender in faith to Christ – and in service for others. As we follow Him, over time we become accountable, responsible, and faithful mature Christians, who bear a great resemblance to the One we call Lord and Teacher!

Keep this in mind… it is easy to adore Christ, but tough to really follow Him!

Chapter 3

Spiritual Life Aglow

Jesus Bids Us Shine[4]

Jesus bids us shine with a clear, pure light,
Like a little candle burning in the night;
In this world of darkness, we must shine,
You in your small corner, and I in mine.

Jesus bids us shine, first of all for Him;
Well He sees and knows it if our light is dim;
He looks down from heaven, sees us shine,
You in your small corner, and I in mine.

Jesus bids us shine, then, for all around,
Many kinds of darkness in this world abound:
Sin, and want, and sorrow—we must shine,
You in your small corner, and I in mine.

---

[4] Susan B. Warner, *pub.*1868

COMMITMENT REQUIRED TO "WIN CHRIST"

"...I consider everything a loss compared to the surpassing greatness of knowing Christ Jesus my Lord, for whose sake I have lost all things. I consider them rubbish, that I may gain (i.e. "win" KJV) Christ...I want to know Christ and the power of his resurrection and the fellowship of sharing his sufferings, becoming like him in death, and so, somehow, to attain to the resurrection from the dead." (Philippians 3:8-10 NIV). That's commitment!

If the local church is to emulate Christ and have an impact on society and culture like the first-century church, in a future filled with even more anti-Christian sentiment, then it must build people who are of one heart and mind (Acts 4:32). This is especially true in their commitment to Jesus Christ as Lord and in fulfilling their Biblical responsibilities to each other. Our secular communities need to see Christ – not flesh – coming from the Body of Christ. **What are our basic Christian commitments and responsibilities?**

Commitment to Jesus Christ as Lord and Savior (Luke 9:23). This refers to the end of life on "my own terms". **Commitment to His Body, the Church.** This means showing our love for Him by loving and fellowshipping with those who are His. "When you did it unto the least of these my brethren, you did it unto me." (Matthew 25:40). **Serving others** is one of Christ's great character qualities and priorities. Christians should highly value it as well (John 13: 14-17). When we see what the Lord has done for us, He moves in our hearts to respond by helping others. He has gifted us with various spiritual gifts to do this (Romans 12 and 1 Corinthians 12) and with other natural or acquired abilities: fix cars, budget money, paint, shop, etc.

We also must follow the leaders God gives us as they follow Christ (i.e. unless they lead us to do or say something or be someone that is unbiblical). See Ephesians 4:11. We need to search the Scriptures (Acts 17:11). The Body of Christ is governed by God ruling through His designated, delegated authority. Authority, however, emanates from relationship. The success of the leader depends heavily upon his ability to love, care, and relate to his people. The leaders God gives us can only exercise authority as people voluntarily submit. (1 Thessalonians 5:12-13). Submission is always voluntary. A disagreement with leaders should always be made with proper, submissive respect for his office. And the leaders should respond with the respect due an ambassador of Christ!

Relating in the Body of Christ is outlined succinctly in Acts 2:42-47 NIV:

- Verse 42 – *"They devoted themselves to the apostles' teaching and to fellowship, to the breaking of bread and to prayer."* We must remember the 30 "one another" scriptures that really define "fellowship" for us. In general, they demonstrate the interdependence between Christians. They also describe times when we need to confront our brethren (e.g. restore, forgive, teach, admonish, and exhort one another).
- Verses 44-45 – *"All believers were together and had everything in common. Selling their possessions and goods, they gave to anyone as he had need."* Christians need to learn that God has set us in the Body to enable everyone's need to be satisfied. This is a very practical part of a Christian's life!
- Verse 46 – *"Every day they continued to meet together in the temple courts. They broke bread in their homes and ate together with glad and sincere hearts."* The commitment was much, much more than just a Sunday or mid-week handshake.
- Verse 47 – *"praising God and enjoying the favor of all the people. And the Lord added to their number daily those*

who were being saved." This way of relating to one another produces results for evangelism.

Here are some things about COMMITMENT that all of us believers need to learn quickly in our Christian lives:

1. Commitment is essential. It's not optional.
2. Commitment is something the Holy Spirit does in each believer's heart (1 Corinthians 12:18, 28). The key for Christians to find their place in a local church is their need for others to stand with them. Unless there's a sense of need, believers probably won't find where they belong (Romans 12:4-5).
3. The Holy Spirit will also move us to share various details of our lives with others. This must always be a voluntary sharing – not something that leaders force church members to do. A safe, trusting environment among members is essential to build relationships in the church for sharing life on a continuous basis. Even with this trust, however, members will still find just an "inner circle" to whom they feel comfortable sharing certain things.
4. Commitment is to the WHOLE Body of Christ worldwide – not just to our local church. Christians need to *"maintain the unity of the Spirit in the bond of peace"* with all believers. (Ephesians 4:3). We participate most actively, however, in our local church's activities and in meeting the needs there.

THANKFULNESS MAKES TENDER HEARTS

As members of the Church, we often ambush and hurt one another. This plays into Satan's plan to get Christians to destroy one another. See Galatians 5: 15. An attitude of gratitude is essential for the Christian's power of spiritual sight. If practiced regularly, we gain a better perspective on the power of Christ's character, how blessed we really are, and how to best expend our spiritual energy. Instead of hurting and ambushing our brothers and sisters in Christ or getting revenge for those who have hurt us, we grow closer to the Lord and resist evil temptations. Instead of ambushing each other, we extend forgiveness. Ephesians 4:32 says, *"Be kind and compassionate to one another, forgiving each other, just as in Christ God forgave you."* That needs to become the normal, expected, behavior of us all!

Thanking and praising our Father brings a peace to our souls like nothing else can. And that peace is then extended to members of His family. We can't be at peace with Him if we are at war with His children. This "war" cuts us off from the support and enjoyment we need that He has provided by giving us a church family.

The devil's deceit and trickery is foiled when we maintain an attitude of gratitude throughout our circumstances. God will turn the tables on him. He will be ambushed by God. In 2 Chronicles 20, we find that the men of Ammon, Moab and Mount Seir were coming to drive the Israelites out of the land God gave them as an inheritance. But Jehoshaphat, king of Judah, appointed men to sing to the Lord and to praise Him for the splendor of His holiness. As they went out at the head of the army, they said, *"Give thanks to the Lord, for His love endures forever."* (verse21). The next verse says, *"As they began to sing and praise, the Lord set* ***ambushes*** *against the men of Ammon and Moab and Mount Seir who were* *invading Judah, and they were defeated."* (verse 22). Let's praise God and ensnare the enemy of our soul.

The Scripture is filled with exhortations to give thanks to the Lord... Deuteronomy 8:10 says, *"When you have eaten and are satisfied, praise the Lord your God for the good land he has given you."* Psalm 100:4-5 says, *"Enter his gates with thanksgiving and his courts with praise; give thanks to him and praise his name. For the Lord is good and his love endures forever; his faithfulness continues through all generations."* Psalm 107:21-22 says, *"Let them give thanks to the Lord for his unfailing love and his wonderful deeds for men. Let them sacrifice thank offerings and tell of his works with songs of joy."*

The Apostle Paul makes joyfully giving thanks in a Christian's life equal in importance with bearing fruit, growing to know God, and being strengthened with all power! Colossians 1:10-12 says, *"And we pray this in order that you may live a life worthy of the Lord and may please him in every way: bearing fruit in every good work, growing in the knowledge of God, being strengthened with all power according to his glorious might so that you may have great endurance and patience, and* ***joyfully giving thanks to the Father****, who has qualified you to share in the inheritance of the saints in the kingdom of light."*

Colossians 3:13-15 is a clear indication that being thankful helps us extend forgiveness to others and to maintain a clear channel for dispensing peace from our hearts. *"Bear with each other and forgive whatever grievances you may have against one another. Forgive as the Lord forgave you. And over all these virtues put on love, which binds them all together in unity. Let the peace of Christ rule in your hearts, since, as members of one body, you were called to peace. And be thankful."* 1 Thessalonians 5:18 says, *"Be joyful always; pray continually; give thanks in all circumstances, for this is God's will for you in Christ Jesus."*

Let's look at ingratitude for a moment. This was Satan's downfall – that's why he keeps trying to ambush us with the same attitude!

Sometimes he gets us to be ungrateful by discouraging us in our circumstances – that's why we are moved by the Holy Spirit to *"encourage one another."* (1 Thessalonians 5:11). Sometimes he tries to separate us from the brethren through pride – that's why we are told, *"Brethren, if a man be overtaken in a fault, ye which are spiritual, restore such a one in the spirit of meekness..."* (Galatians 6:1).

Satan is an expert at these attitudes because it was ingratitude and pride that led to his ruin. He knows what happened to him because of being ungrateful to God and he wants to have the same thing happen to us. Lucifer (i.e. Satan) had so much to give thanks for but he refused. He was created to be beautiful with an internal ability for giving continuous praise to God through music – but instead he rebelled and desired the praise for himself that only God should receive. The key scriptures are Ezekiel 28: 12-17 and Isaiah 16: 12-16.

Jesus was very disturbed with ingratitude. In Luke 17: 11-19, ten men who had leprosy met Him. They called out and asked Jesus to heal them. Jesus told them to go show themselves to the priests. As they were going, all were healed. One of them, a Samaritan, when he saw that he was healed, returned to thank Christ. Then Jesus asked, *"Were not all ten cleansed? Where are the other nine? Was no one found to return and give praise to God except this foreigner?"* There are two points here: First, everyone should have returned to give thanks. Second, those who were "His people" should have been the first ones to give thanks!

God resists those who are ungrateful (i.e. too proud to say thanks). But He gives grace (i.e. unmerited favor) to the humble and thankful. (James 4:6; 1 Peter 5:5). **Therefore, the Church needs to practice thankfulness as a priority – regardless of circumstances.** The Apostle Peter gives a four-fold reason for giving thanks: *"But you are a <u>chosen people</u>, a <u>royal priesthood</u>, a <u>holy nation</u>, a <u>people belonging to God</u>, that you may declare the praises of him who called you out of darkness into his wonderful light."* (1 Peter 2:9). If we practice this behavior, we'll find that giving thanks and praise doesn't mix with ambushing others, holding grudges, or seeking revenge.

THE SIX SPIRITUAL VITAMINS FOR RENEWING THE MIND

The Lord never intended for His Church (i.e. His people) to be hurt from within. The problem is that we're not following His prescription to avoid destructive confrontation. There are three major ingredients to perfectly weaken the flesh (Genesis 17:1) in us that competes with Christ and to stop the ambushes. The first is to adopt a <u>regular diet of the right habits</u> that keep our lives connected to Christ – to really be intimate with *Him.* I like to call these *"*<u>spiritual vitamins</u>*."*

God is a real Person. He feels, He hurts, He wills, He thinks, He enjoys, He hates, etc. He can be known in varying degrees of intimacy. As we live the Christian life, we must ask ourselves, "Do we really want to know Him?" The apostle Paul answered that question for himself. He said, *"...and I count all things but loss for the excellency of the knowledge of Jesus my Lord...That I might know him, and the power of his resurrection, and the fellowship of his sufferings..."* Philippians 3: 8, 10. What's your answer? What's my answer? The truth is that as we desire and seek to know the Lord, we will embrace Christ's values and behaviors. We will be *transformed* from the values and behaviors that previously took precedence in our lives. *"Draw nigh to God, and he will draw nigh to you."* James 4:8. What is your greatest desire? Whatever that is will determine what you become and what you value most. Jesus said, *"For where your treasure is, there your heart will be also."* Matthew 6:21.

Even after we receive Jesus, God keeps calling from the depths of His heart to ours. Jesus said, *"Come unto me all ye that labor and are heavy laden... and <u>learn of me</u>..."* Matthew 11:28-30. God wants us to keep learning of Him – to know Him better and better.

When we come to Christ, our old values come with us. These are of the "natural man" and create weaknesses in us where the devil can get a foothold. Here are a few of the ***old*** values many of us learn to consider very important:

- Be independent. Don't depend on others.
- Take care of yourself – nobody else will
- Lead – don't follow
- Let others serve you. Don't serve anyone.
- Get to know only people who can get you ahead.
- Don't tell people too much about yourself.
- Use people – love things.
- To be respected as a leader, throw your weight around.
- The end justifies the means. Motives don't count.
- Getting is better than giving.

Over time, these values - and resulting behaviors - are transformed to become Christ's values and behaviors. This transformation and learning process, however, requires discipline. In fact, disciplining ourselves is an essential element of living and leading like Christ. The discipline is required to keep us fit and strong in resisting the devil. It allows the Holy Spirit to shape us into Christ's image. Romans 12:1-2.

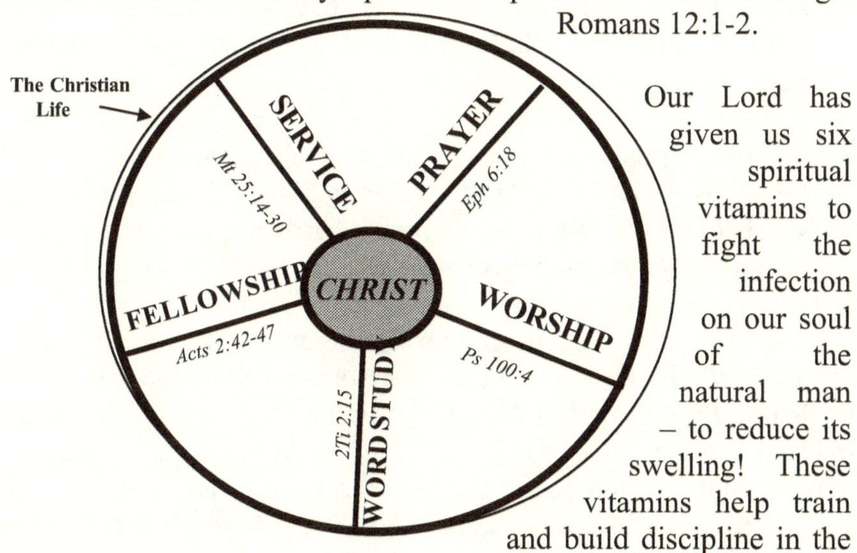

Our Lord has given us six spiritual vitamins to fight the infection on our soul of the natural man – to reduce its swelling! These vitamins help train and build discipline in the

Christian's life. These vitamins can be considered "habits of highly successful Christians." When taken in cooperation with the Holy Spirit, they give us the vigor to follow Christ!

They can be understood best if we first compare the disciplined Christian life to riding a bicycle: The outside rim of the wheel is connected to the hub by means of spokes. The rim is our Christian life. The hub is Christ. We need to keep our life connected to Christ by 5 very important spokes that we can control: Prayer, Bible Study, Worship, Fellowship (the Greek word is "koinonia" which means mutual involvement), and Serving God by using the talents that God has given every Christian. The sixth spoke consists of the trials our Lord allows us to endure. There are struggles for us all – but sometimes we cause our own problems and make the ride "bumpy" for several reasons:

- Christ must be in the center of our lives – the "hub" of the wheel. We often put ourselves back in that place.

- The 5 spokes that we control need to be kept in balance – some of us love to worship regularly - but only study the Word when necessary. Some love to study but sharing their life in fellowship is too "close". Different size spokes cause a rough ride.

- As the 5 spokes get longer, pumping the bike to go forward farther is easier because the wheel is bigger. If the spokes are short, however, we have to pump hard to cover just a short distance because the wheel is small.

God is faithful. The renewing of our mind (Romans 12: 1-2) happens little by little as we discipline ourselves to regularly Study the Word, Pray, Worship, Serve, and Fellowship with our brethren. If just a fraction of the time we waste would be spent doing these things, what a difference it would make for the Kingdom of God. To make our discipline perfect, we go through Trials and

Suffering. The Lord helps and comforts us in them. 2 Corinthians 1:4. The Christian life is not an easy life - but it **is** the abundant life.

We need to be competent and confident in the things of our Lord. We honor the name of our Master Teacher when we are faithful to learn from Him – when we maintain a "teach me" attitude – when we make knowing Him the highest goal of our learning.

As we live the Christian life, we need to make the course of our lives a journey that we savor. Knowing God and being like Christ is our goal. Prayer, Word Study, Worship, Fellowship, Service, and Trials/Suffering are the highways where we will find our Divine Partner and Guide, Jesus Christ. They are the pathways He has carved with His own footprints, the exercise equipment to strengthen and shape us, the light posts to direct our feet, and the "good news shoes" to securely grip the grains of shifting sand littered in our way by the enemy of our souls. They are the spiritual vitamins God has given each of us to help us – by the Holy Spirit – to know Him and emulate Him.

So then, here is a way to remember to take your spiritual vitamins – the six habits of highly successful Christians:

Vitamin A – Ask – *Prayer*
Vitamin B – Bible – *Study the Word*
Vitamin C – Comfort – *Comfort others with the comfort He gives us*
Vitamin D – Do – *Service*
Vitamin E – Exalt – *Worship*
Vitamin K – Koinonia –*Fellowship*

"*My soul longeth, yea, even fainteth for the courts of the Lord: my heart and my flesh crieth out for the living God...Blessed is the man whose strength is in thee; in whose heart are the highways to Zion.*" (Psalm 84: 2, 5 RV)

CHRIST'S SUPPLEMENTS FOR THE SOUL

How can we avoid playing into Satan's plan for Christians to destroy one another? How can we avoid destructive confrontation in the Church? We need to keep our eyes on Jesus –the Lamb of God. What did He leave us as a legacy of values and behaviors to emulate? How can we be the ambassadors of His grace and positively influence lives like He does? To "gain Christ" (Philippians 3: 10), we need to emulate His character and adopt His priorities. We must embrace His values – His supplements for the soul (i.e. our emotions, intellect, and will)." Here they are:

SERVING OTHERS. We Christians need to value serving others. It's a supplement for the soul's **will.** I like to say this is the self-sacrifice of the cross. See John 3:16. Jesus said, *"He who is greatest among you will be your servant."* (Matthew 23:11). At another occasion, before His crucifixion, Jesus laid aside His garments, wrapped a towel around Himself, and began washing the disciples feet and wiping them with the towel. When He finished, He said to them, *"... If I, then, your Lord and Teacher have washed your feet, you also ought to wash one another's feet. For I have given you an example that you should do as I have done...If you know these things, happy are you if you do them."* (John 13:13-17). Jesus also said, at another time, *"Whoever desires to be first among you, let him be your slave – just as the Son of Man did not come to be served, but to serve, and to give His life a ransom for many."* (Matthew 20:27-28).

HEART-TO-HEART. The second value is called heart-to-heart. It's a supplement for the soul's **emotions**. It's the love of the cross. See Romans 5:8. It's placing importance upon getting to know the people God has given us or placed us among and allowing them get to know us as well. We need to "feel the heartbeat" of people. Many Christians forget the whole reason Jesus came to earth. It wasn't just to save us. Thank God that He restored a right relationship with our Heavenly Father by paying the price of death for our sin.

He also came, however, so we could get our arms around God – to "hug Him". The world had lost its knowledge of God – then, like now, there were many ideas about what God was like. Jesus said, *"He who has seen me, has seen the Father."* (John 14:9). Jesus always valued taking the time to get to know people and to meet their needs. Remember blind Bartemaeus. Jesus was headed for Jerusalem. And when Bartemaeus heard that it was Jesus of Nazereth who was passing by, he called out to Him, *"Jesus, thou son of David, have mercy on me."* (Luke 18: 38). His disciples told the old man to keep still and not bother the Master. But Jesus wanted to know this man's heart. He said, *"What wilt thou that I do unto thee?"*

Zacchaeus was another who wanted to get to know Jesus – and he wasn't disappointed. Jesus looked up into the tree, where this corrupt tax collector had positioned himself to catch a glimpse of the Master, and said, "*Zacchaeus, make haste, and come down; for today I must abide at your house."* (Luke 19: 5)

As far as getting to know us, Jesus said, *"I am the good shepherd, and I know My sheep and am known by My own."* (John 10:14). Speaking of the good shepherd, Jesus said, *"To him the doorkeeper opens; and the sheep hear his voice; and he calls his own sheep by name and he leads them out."* (John 10:3). Jesus knows what it's like to be you and me. He cares about our every concern. He even cares enough to have every hair on each of our heads numbered. (Matthew 10:30)

We too need to value being heart-to-heart with the people our Lord has given to us and placed us among. This value is vitally important in the area of confronting our brothers and sisters in Christ – when it is necessary to confront them after they've hurt us. Heart-to-heart is also especially important for church leaders to embrace with church members if they are to maintain effective church discipline.

WISDOM FROM ABOVE. This is a supplement for the soul's **intellect**. James 3:17 says that, *"The wisdom that is from above is first pure, then peaceable, gentle, willing to yield, full of mercy and good fruits (i.e. some translations say goodness, fairness, genuineness), without partiality, and without hypocrisy."* Like Jesus, we need to value these qualities – primarily being pure. It's the holiness of the cross. See 2 Corinthians 5:21. We need to have pure motives and be a person that can be trusted by others to help them through the "storms" of their lives. Thy want someone with integrity. If we want to help others – to have them share with us their troubles and seek the insights God gives us – then we must also have pure motives and this wisdom from above.

We should examine our hearts for this wisdom which is first pure. The way to do that well is to let our Lord Jesus Christ take us on an incredible journey through our hearts. Consider what our Lord might say as He enters all the rooms there. See *My Heart, Christ's Home* by Robert Boyd Munger, 1986. For example, what would He see in the **Study Room** (i.e. your mind)? What are the magazines, books, TV programs we read? He would want His picture in the center of that room and the books of the Scriptures on all the book shelves because a mind is in perfect peace which is stayed on Him. Isaiah 26:3. What would you serve Jesus in the **Dining Room** of your heart? What are your appetites and desires? Are they your education, wealth, investments, awards, etc.? If so, Jesus would not eat much and would say, *"I have meat that you know not of – to do the will of my Father who sent me and to finish His work"* (John 4:34).

So besides valuing serving others and being heart-to heart with them, the Lord wants us to appreciate and embrace this wisdom from above which is first pure.

PULL – DON'T - PUSH. This is again a supplement for the soul's **will**. I like to call it the humility and obedience of the cross. See Philippians 2: 8. We shouldn't be twisting our people's arms to make them do something – or backing them into a corner or making them feel guilty or manipulating them into submission. That's not Christ. If we're to emulate Christ, then we need to learn to draw them to us – and eventually to Christ. In Matthew 7:11, Jesus says, *"Come unto me all you..."* He draws us to Himself. Even when His requirements seem difficult, we do what He wants because He's everything we want to be – and as we follow Him, we become like Him.

The path that leads to emulating Christ takes us through the cross. We can't take a shortcut. Jesus resisted the temptation to "take a short cut" and avoid the cross three times. Luke 22:44, Matthew 16:21-23, Matthew 4:8-9. ***If we want to be Christlike Christians, resist the devil, and run the Christian race effectively, maintaining unity in the body of Christ, we must embrace the values we find in the Christ of the cross.***

ANOTHER ORDINARY CHRISTMAS!

Within the Church, God uses ordinary people to do extraordinary things. That's because it's not by our might, nor by our power, but by His Spirit that the real work is done. Every believer is *"in Christ Jesus, who has become for us wisdom from God – that is, our righteousness, holiness and redemption. Therefore, as it is written: 'Let him who boasts boast in the Lord.'"* See 1 Corinthians 1: 30-31. Also, the Holy Spirit is resident in each believer. See John 14: 16-17 and Acts 2. The Lord has given every believer spiritual gifts to use for benefiting the whole Church. See 1 Corinthians 12: 4-7. As each of us does the work God has assigned us to do, the Body of Christ *"grows and builds itself up in love."* See Ephesians 4: 13-16. In that way our Lord has made all of us dependent upon Him and every other believer. See 1 Corinthians 12: 21-26. God has done this *"so that there should be no division in the body, but that its parts should have equal concern for each other. If one part suffers, every part suffers with it; if one part is honored, every part rejoices with it."* See 1 Corinthians 12: 25-26.

I've been thinking this Christmas about how our Lord seeks out those who are the most unlikely, ordinary people to carry out His extraordinary work. He takes ordinary people and makes them part of His royal family – children of God and heirs like the elder son. *"But when the time had fully come, God sent his Son, born of a woman, born under the law, to redeem those under the law, that we might receive the full rights of sons. Because you are sons, God sent the Spirit of his Son into our hearts, the Spirit who calls out, 'Abba, Father.' So you are no longer a slave, but a son; and since you are a son, God has made you also an heir."* See Galatians 4: 4-7. So God will *"meet all your needs according to his glorious riches in Christ Jesus."* See Philippians 4: 19.

He also takes us ordinary people and makes us ambassadors of Christ. Equipped with the indwelling Holy Spirit, He leads us to reach out to Christ – *"Put your finger here; see my hands. Reach out your hand and put it into my side. Stop doubting and believe."* John 20:27. We reach out to one another – *"I tell you the truth, whatever you did for one of the least of these brothers of mine, you did for me."* Matthew 25:40. We reach out to the lost – *"...go and make disciples of all nations, ...and teaching them to obey everything I have commanded you."* Matthew 28:19, 20. We learn to reach higher – *"For as the heavens are higher than the earth, so are my ways higher than your ways, and my thoughts than your thoughts."* Isaiah 55:9. We learn to reach deeper – *"The Spirit searches all things, even the deep things of God."* 1 Corinthians 2:10. We learn to reach ahead - *"Forgetting those things that are behind, and reaching forth unto those things that are before..."* Philippians 3:13. We press to reach our goal - *"I press on toward the goal to win the prize (i.e Christ) for which God has called me heavenward in Christ Jesus."* Philippians 3: 8, 14

He used murderers, idol worshippers, and the poor - among others – to demonstrate His love, grace, power, and riches. The Apostle Paul, having imprisoned and killed the Lord's early converts, was the least likely to send the message of God's love and grace. It confounds our logic that Moses, having committed murder, should bring us God's righteous laws. Gideon, who was the son of an idol worshipper, was used to bring victory against the overwhelming forces of the Medianites. See Judges 6 and 7. God even used the poor widow of Zarephath, who was about to die of starvation along with her son, to sustain Elijah – the prophet who never died. See 1 Kings 17:9.

And we remember at Christmas time an unlikely, ordinary woman, a virgin who brought forth a Child, who would be called *"God with us"* and *"Jesus"*, because He would save His people from their sins. This Child became the One and Only Salvation and Hope of all mankind. One who would take upon Himself the sins of the whole world as a Perfect and Sinless Sacrifice to satisfy

God's sentence of death that was over everyone because all had sinned. See Romans 5: 12. He would also be resurrected from the dead to give new life to all who believe in Him. God didn't use royalty or a prophetess. He didn't use the wealthy or the strong. He chose a young woman who would – as a living sacrifice - surrender herself and become "perfectly weak" to the Holy Spirit, who would overshadow her and produce something that only God could do in her life!

You and I are also ordinary, unlikely sinners, saved by God's G.R.A.C.E - **G**od's **R**iches **A**t **C**hrist's **E**xpense. We are asked to *"surrender ourselves as living sacrifices unto God ...and be not conformed to the pattern of this world, but be transformed by the renewing of our minds..."* See Romans 12: 1-2. Let's respond in faith, as Mary and many others have done, and adjust our lives to be perfectly weak in the flesh (See Gen 17:1) so that the Holy Spirit in us can produce through us something only He can do!! **F**orsaking **A**ll **I** **T**rust **H**im – F.A.I.T.H!

"FORGETTING WHAT IS BEHIND…I PRESS ON…"

As each new year unfolds, what is the central theme of the book our lives will write? What will our friends, neighbors, workmates, schoolmates, and our brethren say about us when the year ends? More importantly, what will our Lord Jesus Christ say about us? As I asked myself these questions, I recalled Paul's words to the saints at Philippi: *"I consider everything a loss compared to the surpassing greatness of knowing Christ Jesus my Lord…that I may* ***gain*** *Christ…becoming like him in his death, and so, somehow, to attain to the resurrection of the dead…Not that I have already obtained all this…But one thing I do: Forgetting what is behind and straining toward what is ahead, I press toward the goal to win the prize…"* Philippians 3: 8 – 14. The Prize he spoke about was Christ – being like Christ! That means surrendering ourselves as living sacrifices to God (Romans 12: 1-2) so He can make us into servant-leaders, who are in the image of His Son.

All believers are simultaneously leaders and servants. We are commissioned by the Lord as disciple-makers (Matthew 28: 19-20) and as His ambassadors (2 Corinthians 5:20). We, therefore, have influence over many people with whom God sets us. At the same time, we are called to follow and serve as His minister-priests (Revelation 5:10). As God told Elijah to anoint Elisha (1 Kings 19:16, 19) to take his place, similarly He gave Jesus direction and authority to anoint every believer. As Elijah cast his mantle upon Elisha, so Christ casts the mantle of the Holy Spirit upon every believer. Just as Elisha, who wanted a double portion of Elijah's spirit, was required to keep his eyes upon Elijah, likewise we go in the power of the Holy Spirit, and we keep our minds stayed upon our great High-Priest, Servant Leader, who is the Lamb upon the throne. In 2004, let's offer ourselves – without restraint – to being used in both the leader and servant roles – but especially as His servant to others!

The Great Fisher of Men leads us often into deep waters where only Christ's outstretched, nail-driven hands provide the strength to keep serving others. We learn that it was not the nails that held Christ to the cross, but rather His love for the Father and us. Through it all, He presses into us the servant-leader qualities of self-sacrifice, faithfulness, endurance, patience, and love. Listen to what Jesus says about learning to serve: "Just as the Son of Man did not come to be served, but to serve, and to give His life a ransom for many." Matthew 20:28. *"For who is greater, he who sits at the table, or he who serves? Is it not he who sits at the table? But I am among you as the One who serves."* Luke 22:27. *"If I then, your Lord and Teacher, have washed your feet, you also ought to wash one another's feet. For I have given you an example, that you should do as I have done to you."* John 13:14-15.

We are leader – pilgrims in the world wearing the mantle of the Holy Spirit. And as long as the natural man lives in us, he (the natural man) is being progressively reduced so that Christ might increase. While we serve others here, we are in training for a wondrous assignment He has prepared for us – to rule and reign with Him throughout eternity! Scripture tells us that the resurrected and raptured believers are dressed in glorious white robes (e.g. mantles) in heaven. We are told that after the rapture of the Church (1 Thessalonians 4: 14-17) – which could happen at any time – at the Judgment Seat of Christ, we will receive crowns; also, that we will lay them at the feet of Christ. See 2 Corinthians 5:10 and Revelation 4: 10-11.

In place of these crowns, we will receive a mantle of light – Mount of Transfiguration light – that we carry throughout eternity and *"shine as the brightness of the firmament...as stars for ever and ever."* Daniel 12:3. *"They (e.g. us) will see His face, and His name will be on their foreheads...They will not need the light of a lamp or the light of the sun, for the Lord God will give them light.*

And they shall reign for ever and ever." Revelation 22: 4-5. I believe that the name of Christ that will be on our foreheads is "The Light of the World"!

One day we – with Elijah, Moses, Paul and all the other raptured believers – will return with Christ to defeat the Antichrist and the armies gathered at the Battle of Armageddon (Revelation 19: 11-16). We will follow the great Light of the World – the Sun of Righteousness – who will be clothed in a mantle of brilliant smaller stars that will be flowing behind Him as every eye beholds the return of Christ. Then what God told Abraham thousands of years earlier will be literally true: *"He (God) took him (Abraham) outside and said, 'Look up at the heavens and count the stars – if indeed you can count them.' Then He said to him, 'So shall your offspring be.'"*

Be ready! Press on for the Prize by being yielded servant-leaders who are being shaped in Christ's image. Especially serve others like the Master! We could see Him face-to-face this year!

CHRISTIANS WITHOUT BORDERS

We Christians need to be "without borders" when it comes to helping others – we'll go anywhere, do anything, make any sacrifice for leading someone to Christ. I was privileged to travel 18 hours by air and then 12 hours by bus over two mountains at my own expense to teach 110 pastors/Christian workers in the Philippines about Christlike leadership. There is a group called "Doctors Without Borders", who travel wherever they are needed to bring God's love through healing.

We should not, however, be Christians "without borders" when it comes to our values and behaviors. God sets the standards for our living. We shouldn't be blending with everyone so much that we look like the rest of the world! Jesus said, *"If you belonged to the world, it would love you as its own. As it is, you do not belong to the world, but I have chosen you out of the world. That is why the world hates you."* John 15: 19. He said, *"You are the light of the world."* Matthew 5:14. Our character qualities and priorities, as well as our behavior, must be guided by the Holy Spirit. And no doubt – because we are so different - that will bring us persecution as it did Christ.

This reminds me of the unique kind of race we are running. We are gently drawn onward by the Holy Spirit, who always encourages us to run it God's way:

Because Satan tries to deceive Christians concerning what the real abundant Christian life is all about, the Holy Spirit asks, "What track are you on? Is it the 'great career track?' Is it the 'ego building track?' Is it the 'material possessions or investment track?'" "Or are you", He reminds us, "on the high-calling track?" This is the narrow track – the course that's marked out by the example of Christ and leads to being shaped into His image. Philippians 3:14. The racetrack is full of obstacles – many peaks and valleys – many things that cause runners to stumble, scrap their arms and legs. The Holy Spirit reminds us that Jesus never leaves or forsakes us. He will not let us go through any suffering without Him. He's the one who asks us to come unto Him when we labor and are heavy-laden, to learn of Him, because He is meek and lowly of heart and will give us rest. Matthew 11:28.

The Holy Spirit asks, "Is Jesus Lord of your life? Does He own the deed to your heart, or is He just a guest there?" "What equipment are you wearing? Is it the armor of God that includes having *"our feet shod with the preparation of the gospel of peace"*; or are we wearing shoes with pointed tips that hurt our fellow runners?" The Holy Spirit asks us, "How are you running – by faith or by sight?" *"Without faith it is impossible to please him: for he that cometh to God must believe that he is, and that he is a rewarder of them that diligently seek him."* Hebrews 11:6. He reminds us that *"all things work together for good to them that love God, to them who are the called according to his purpose."* Romans 8:28.

How are you moving? Are you crawling, walking, or running when it comes to Christian growth? Runners kick hardest when they "see" the finish line. You may be crawling and not running well because you have a "fuzzy" view of the finish line of our faith (i.e. Christ). Has the Holy Spirit ever asked you about who wins this Christian race? Do you try to beat me to the finish line? Do Christians compete with each other to win? No, that should never be the case. This is a team race where we all win together! We finish the race together and we are always about Father's business to help one another finish well! *"Even when we were dead in sins, hath (God) quickened us together with Christ (by grace ye are saved); And hath raised us up together, and made us sit together in heavenly places in Christ Jesus"* Ephesians 2: 5-6.

Whenever I'm reminded of "who wins" and helping each other win, the Holy Spirit reminds me about the *"cloud of witnesses"* in

Hebrews 12:1. Who are the people that are the great cloud of witnesses in our lives? Is it just the Bible heroes of the faith? I don't believe they are the only heroes. When you're sitting in church with brothers and sisters in Christ, look around you. You'll find heroes of the faith there too. As *"the Lord went before them by day in a pillar of cloud to show them the way"* (Exodus 13:21), God also uses us Christians to help show one another the way as we faithfully study and share His Word.

The Holy Spirit always wants us to remember the Prize for which we're running. Is it heaven? Is it to prosper here on earth? Is it to get the best mansion in heaven? Is it to get one of the five crowns? No, it's none of those things. The Prize is Christ – to be like Him – *"to know him, the power of His resurrection and the fellowship of his sufferings"* Philippians 3:10. Jesus is the Prize of the high calling of God!

Running the race looking backwards doesn't work. Past accomplishments can become an anchor. We can be guided by the past – like a rudder. Better yet, I want to keep my eyes forward and my body straining toward the marked out track. *"...but this one thing I do, forgetting what is behind, and reaching forth unto those things that are before, I press toward the mark for the prize of the high calling of God in Christ Jesus."* Philippians 3: 13-14.

Let's be Christians "without borders" who run the race of life God's way – staying within the boundaries of Christ's values and behaviors.

GROWING TOGETHER IN CHRIST

I've been thinking about the Church and how important it is for us to grow together in Christ. ***Growing*** means becoming more like Christ (i.e. becoming a mature Christian). Knowing Christ and being Christlike is the goal (or the Prize) of the Christian life. Paul said that his objective in life was to "gain" Christ (Philippians 3:8) – everything else he considered to be garbage. Not just to accept Him as Savior and Lord but to experience and know Christ intimately in the fellowship of His sufferings and the power of His resurrection. Philippians 3: 10. Our love relationship with Christ means everything. It is how we know Him, His ways, and His purposes. Paul said, *"Brothers, I do not consider myself yet to have taken hold of it (i.e. gaining Christ). But one thing I do: Forgetting what is behind and straining toward what is ahead, I press on toward the goal to win the prize (i.e. Christ) for which God has called me heavenward in Christ Jesus."* Philippians 3: 13.

Growing Together means growing closer to one another in the unity of the Spirit. Before His crucifixion and resurrection, Jesus gave us a new commandment that we should love one another as He loved us. He also said by that love, others would know that we were His disciples – that we belonged to Him and no other. John 13: 34-35. He prayed to our Heavenly Father that the Church (i.e. all His disciples) would be one - as He was one with the Father, that we would be one together. There was an important reason for maintaining this unity. Jesus said it this way, *"May they also be (one) in us so that the world may believe that you have sent me."* John 17: 21. In other words, our unity as believers has an evangelistic purpose to draw people to Christ!

Growing Together also means being together for helping each other grow more like Christ. The Scripture is replete with instructions for the brethren to help each other. I think there are 30 "one another" verses in the New Testament. Here are some examples: *"Accept one another..."* Romans 15:7; *"Be devoted to one another in brotherly love. Honor one another above yourselves."* Romans 12:10. *"Live in harmony with one another."* Romans 12: 16. *Bear ye one another's burdens..."* Galatians 6:2. *"...pray for each other so that you may be healed."* James 5:16.

Growing Together In Christ means growing with all the essentials provided by Christ. Just like Isaac was automatically born rich as Abraham's son, so also we who are in Christ are already rich. We don't have to earn our salvation or work to be rich because *"...my God will supply all your needs according to his glorious riches in Christ Jesus."* Philippians 4: 19. *"It is because of him (i.e. God) that you are in Christ Jesus, who has become for us wisdom from God – that is, our righteousness, holiness and redemption."* 1 Corinthians 1: 30. Our being "in Christ" by God's will and design means that wherever Christ went, we went with Him – to the cross for our sin problem; to the grave and resurrection for living a new life; to heaven with Him to sit at our Father's right hand and become citizens there. Not only are we in Christ, but Christ – by the Holy Spirit – is in us. For that reason, we have the power to overcome our problems moment-by-moment and day-by-day. We can be over-comers NOW and in our future!

The church can't function without our ***Growing Together in Christ***. It functions as one unit with spiritual leaders and members. All of us are interdependent – we need each other. Each leader and member needs the others to fully know God's will. Each leader has a responsibility to equip the members. Ephesians 4: 11-13, 16 says that God gives leaders to help members become like Christ; and also to help members do meaningful work for others so the church grows and builds itself up in love. Each member has a role. Galatians 6:1-5 says that role is to fulfill the law of Christ to love others as He loved us; to help fallen brethren by bearing their burdens; and, to check our own actions using Scripture as the standard. The pastor is responsible for the church and to the church. For the church – so members develop a close relationship with God. To the church – so he fulfills his responsibilities and is fairly compensated.

Because a church is the body of Christ, it functions best when spiritual leaders and members together share what they sense God wants the church to be and do. A church needs to hear the whole counsel of God through both its leaders and members. Then it can proceed in confidence and in unity to do God's will. So church leadership needs to encourage everyone to share how God is guiding him/her. By sharing our thoughts with each other, it helps someone else encounter the Lord in a meaningful way; and for the body to grow together in Christ!

PERFECTLY WEAK

At first glance, it seems like these two words – perfectly weak - don't go together. Either we're perfect, which means we are strong mentally, physically, emotionally, OR we are weak in those same areas. So how can we be perfectly weak? The answer to that question comes from what Jesus said to the Apostle Paul – *"...for My strength is made perfect in weakness."* And in Paul's own words, *"When I am weak, then I am strong.*" See 2 Corinthians 12:9-10. But how can Paul say he is both weak and strong? The patriarch of our faith, Abraham, was made aware of what it means. God didn't speak to Abraham for 13 years after he had Ishmael, a son by his own flesh – his natural strength. After 13 tears of silence, God then said to him, *"Walk before me and be thou perfect."* See Genesis 17:1. Did God mean be perfect in your natural abilities? Did God mean be perfect in your good deeds? Did God mean be perfectly strong, smart, and stable?

No. God didn't mean any of these things. God waited until Abraham's natural strength had dissipated – especially concerning implanting a seed in Sara to have a child. Neither Sara nor Abraham could have a child by their own natural ability. God was saying, "When you had Ishmael your natural strength got the glory! But now ***surrender your weak and imperfect flesh to me as a living sacrifice, be completely dependent upon me, and allow Me to give you My strength – walk as one who is perfectly weak!"***

God asks us to walk that way with Him too! He wants us to walk, maintaining a "new wine skin" heart – one that is trusting and pliable – for Him to transform us into the image of Christ, and work through us to touch others. Hear what Romans 12: 1-2 says, *"Therefore, I urge you, brothers, in view of God's mercy, to offer yourselves as living sacrifices, holy and pleasing to God – which is your spiritual worship. Do not conform any longer to the pattern of this world, but be transformed by the renewing of your mind."* When we wait upon the Lord in this way, then throughout eternity God will get the glory, honor, and praise for ***His*** work in and through us.

Our Lord Jesus Christ has given us these "spiritual vitamins" to transform us and make us perfectly weak:

† Vitamin A – **Ask**. This vitamin is Prayer. We need to meet the Lord daily in the living room of our hearts beside the hearth, where He's always ready to hear our burdens and minister to us.

† Vitamin B – **Bible**. This vitamin is Study the Word. The Lord wants the "study room" of our hearts (i.e. our minds) to have the 66 books of the Bible on the bookshelves so He can quickly bring His Word to our understanding in all situations. He also wants a picture of Himself from His Word in the center of our mind.

† Vitamin C – **Comfort.** This vitamin is comforting others with the comfort God comforts us with when we suffer (2 Corinthians 1:4). God never wastes anything. He uses all our experiences to show us how dependent we are on Him and to use us to show His love to others.

† Vitamin D – **Do**. This vitamin is allowing Him to use us in a service for His kingdom. He has bestowed gifts on all of us and He expects us to produce fruit from them. What department in our Father's business are you in?

† Vitamin E – **Exalt**. This vitamin is worship. And there's a nutrient that goes with worship known as gratitude. It gives us a better perspective on the power of Christ's character, how blessed we really are, and how to best expend our spiritual energy. We grow closer to our Lord and resist evil temptations.

- † Vitamin K – **Koinonia**. That's a Greek word for fellowship with other Christians. The rebirth we have through Christ's blood, made us new creations who need one another to grow effectively.

To become **PERFECTLY WEAK**, we need to take these vitamins as prescribed by our Great Physician - in equal shares and with increasing dosages as we continue walking with Him.

GOT GRIEF?

Have you got grief? Do your trials and suffering seem overwhelming? I've just gone through the second biggest trial of my life. I recently had open heart surgery, where a valve in my heart had to be repaired. It meant 17 days at Deborah Heart and Lung Center, as well as a long recovery. At the same time that was happening, my beloved father passed away. I couldn't even attend his funeral. But God was faithful to me. He not only gave me a new healthy heart, but He arranged – just prior to entering the hospital - for me to lead my Dad to Christ. He also allowed the funeral service to be a beautiful testimony to my Dad and his salvation through Christ. And the service was done, without my intervention, by the perfect pastor-friend of mine.

Satan tried to derail the service and discourage me – as he may do to you - but God saw me through it all. And God will help you overcome as well! Remember, *"There has no temptation (i.e. grief or trial) taken you but such as is common to man: but God is faithful, who will not suffer you to be tempted above that ye are able; but will with the temptation also make a way of escape, that ye may be able to bear it."* 1 Corinthians 10:13.

My other biggest trial was when my wife left me on our 25th wedding anniversary to be with another man – even though I had been faithful to her and - by most people's standards - a good provider for my family. She left just three months after my dear Mom died from cancer. She wouldn't even try seeing a counselor with me to reconcile. That suffering seemed too much to carry! All I could hear at first was something like, "How can someone as wounded and inadequate as you expect to overcome such an enormous mountain of grief?" But God was faithful to me again! The answer was by taking one step at a time, that's how! Until this happened, the only time I studied God's Word was for teaching my weekly adult Sunday school class. And the only time I worshipped and prayed was in my car going to work. But the Lord taught me to put Him and His kingdom first – not to just "fit Him into my schedule" but to rearrange my schedule to make time with Him most important. As I did that, little by little, my Sunday school students told me my teaching was so much more powerful and effective than before! And, little by little, I met and married someone who has supported my teaching ministry and also encouraged me to become an author for the Lord!

I faced the open heart surgery, my dad & mom's death, and my wife leaving me – by depending upon my Precious Lord! Look to Jesus, the Author and Finisher of our faith. Remember to be *"careful (i.e. anxious) for nothing, but in everything by prayer and supplication with thanksgiving let your requests be made know unto God."* Philippians 4:6. Remember, *"My God shall supply all your need according to His riches in glory by Christ Jesus."* Philippians 4: 19. I suspect that, if we could see through God's eyes the reason and end result for the trial – the precious jewels we're becoming - we'd praise and thank Him.

Even when we are obedient to the Lord, the dark shadows in our lives may not clear right away. Sometimes things even seem to get worse before they get better. But God's grace – His unmerited favor towards us – will get us through. Be encouraged by Psalm 34: 15-19 where David said, *"The eyes of the Lord are on the righteous and his ears are attentive to their cry...The righteous cry out, and the Lord hears them; he delivers them from all their troubles. The Lord is close to the brokenhearted and saves those who are crushed in spirit. A righteous man may have many troubles, but the Lord delivers him from them all..."*

Let's also not be so fixed upon our trials that we forget how blessed we really are – remember all the benefits we have in Christ. I recently read this little verse in *Our Daily Bread*: "As you travel down life's pathway, may this be ever your goal: Keep your eye upon the doughnut, and not upon the hole!" Our grief is the hole, but Christ and His benefits are the "sweetness."

Psalm 147 refers to God as the one who *"counts the number of the stars; He calls them all by name."* But while it highlights God's power, it also tells us that this awesome Creator of the universe is the most caring person we could ever know: *"He heals the brokenhearted...lifts up the humble...takes pleasure in those who fear him, in those who hope in his mercy."* Psalm 147: 3-11.

So have you got grief? Then, *"Trust in the Lord with all thine heart; and lean not unto thine own understanding. In all thy ways acknowledge him (i.e. bring Him into your circumstances), and he shall direct thy paths."* Proverbs 3: 5-6.

Chapter 4

Wounded By Friendly Fire

Handle with Care[5]

Look out, little woman! Look out, little man!
Do be just as careful as ever you can,
For each of you carry a treasure too rare
To risk any trifling, so "Handle with care!"

Your soul is the treasure, and day after day
You choose which to follow: the straight or broad way;
So mind what comes nigh you, and heed where you go—
Your soul is eternal for weal or for woe.

The words of the Savior were "Come unto Me!"
So sweetly He spoke them in dear Galilee;
He wants us to serve Him with pure hearts, and true;
Then let us be careful in all that we do.

Refrain:
Look out! Look out, little woman!
Look out, little man!

---

[5] Judith Garnett

"SHIFTING SAINTS" – MY HEART'S PLEA

In 1998, George Barna, Barna Research Group, in ***"Profiles of American Churches"***, said that twenty percent of church-goers change their church in a typical year. He also said that fifteen to twenty percent of church-goers attend more than one church on a rotating basis. On December 17, 2002, Mr. Barna wrote ***"Seven Paradoxes Regarding America's Faith"***. In that article he notes, "Study after study emphasizes that we make assumptions about people's spiritual understanding that are unjustified. The American Church desperately needs a back-to-basics movement to fill in the cracks in our spiritual understanding."

Despite the fact that pastors say evangelism and outreach rank as the top priorities of their churches, the proportion of both non-Christians and unchurched adults have remained unchanged since 2000. "In fact, because the population has increased, the number of unchurched and non-Christian people in the nation has actually grown", says Barna. Please hear what the Spirit is saying to the churches. **We are losing the battle for souls in America.**

My experience confirms these results. In 32 years as a born-again believer, family relocations have brought me to seven churches from 5 different denominations in 3 States and Europe. They've all had many "transplants." Unsuspecting, unprepared Christians, who should be making disciples, are licking their wounds and wandering around looking for their perception of a real "New Testament" home church – only to be disillusioned again and again! When will the Body of Christ realize its influence is being progressively weakened from within by friendly fire? When will the spiritual "wheat" stop being contaminated by the "tares" sown by the enemy of our souls?

As a Christian educator for over 27 years, workshop leader, keynoter, and as president of New Jersey Christian Ministries - a 46-year old, non-profit, inter-denominational teaching arm of the Church with 90 instructors - I am well aware of spiritual "ambushes" throughout the Body of Christ. We consistently minister annually to about 1500 adults and teens, including over 400 teachers and 200 church leaders from 160-240 different churches/ministries. We do this through a Christian Ministries Convention and smaller regional events in New Jersey.

The Church needs to learn Satan's game plan for deceiving, dividing and destroying Christians – how Christians ambush one another and their pastor - how pastors ambush their people – and how some churches act like cults. They also need a back-to-basics understanding of God's plan for them to avoid these destructive confrontations in the church – to maintain the unity of the Spirit in the bond of peace. They need to know what it means to make Jesus Lord and trust Him, walk with Him, and commit to a local church and serve one another.

My heart, as a Christian leader and teacher, is inexorably connected to this struggle. Though I am concerned for all believers around the globe, my heart's cry is for the American Church to be unified within each local church and throughout the Body of Christ in our battle for souls. It's God's plan for Christians to avoid destructive confrontation and make a meaningful commitment to a local church.

The Lord wants to change the course of "shifting saints" from a desperate search for the right church to the passionate pursuit of making disciples. Please consider seriously what the Spirit is sharing with us in this article. Also, if you've been wounded in the "house of your friends" (i.e. God's House), please pray for unity in the American Church.

CRIMINAL CHURCH INVESTIGATION (CCI)

Have you noticed all the TV shows, with their policemen, detectives, and lawyers, dealing with criminals and breaking the law? Two of the most popular are Law & Order and CSI. There's Law & Order, Law & Order Special Victims Unit, and Law & Order Criminal Intent. There's CSI, CSI Miami, and CSI New York. And in most shows, the bad guys are brought to justice.

Have you ever wished that the Church had its law enforcement officers - people whose responsibility was to promote law & order, which spiritually we call righteousness? After all, the Lord told everyone who belongs to Him to *"seek first the kingdom of God and His righteousness..."* Matthew 6: 33. Do you seek righteousness? Don't you wish everyone did? Unfortunately, the Church is full of spiritual criminals – "wolves in sheep's clothing" who ambush Christians and drive 15% - 20% of them out of their churches every year looking for what they consider a real New Testament church – only to be disillusioned again and again. Sadly, maybe you know some of these people; or maybe you and I have been these spiritual criminals.

There are many episodes of Spiritual Law & Order. Being ambushed by the "crime" of slander in the Church is just one of them. Ephesians 4:31. If you've been ambushed by slander, then you've met **Rep Torn.** When I met him he was recently married. He needed a job to support his wife and a child they expected some day. So Helpful Hand decided to intercede for him with a company that was doing work for Helpful Hand's employer. Because of his influence, they hired Rep Torn. Helpful Hand also arranged for another member of his church, Grateful Youth, to be hired. Rep Torn and Grateful Youth then worked together. Helpful Hand would give Rep Torn a ride to and from work whenever it was needed. He even gave him and his wife a vacation at his summer house. Rep Torn was not very good at his job but his employer kept him on to show respect for Helpful Hand. After a while, however, when there were cutbacks, Rep Torn and Grateful Youth had to be let go. Their employer, however, gave them plenty of notice to get other jobs. While they waited, Rep Torn began discrediting Helpful Hand's reputation to Grateful Youth – telling him how Helpful Hand wasn't doing enough for them - and other disparaging remarks.

After they were terminated, Rep Torn and Helpful Hand were in the back of the church. Rep Torn began blaming Helpful Hand for Grateful Youth not attending church any more. He became very loud – with many other church members around them – and said it was Helpful Hand who was responsible for this because he hadn't saved their jobs. Rep Torn became so emotional that some people went to get the pastor, who eventually had him come in for counseling. After that, Helpful Hand wondered if those who over heard the argument ever received his Sunday School teaching any more. Did they believe Rep Torn's slander?

Young's Compact Bible Dictionary says that <u>slander</u> means making false statements that harm or malign a person's reputation. If it is against God, it is called blasphemy. The ninth commandment concerns the bearing of false witness (Exodus 20:16). It is many times condemned in the New Testament by the Apostles (e.g. 2 Corinthians 12:20; Ephesians 4:31; 1 Peter 2:1). The one who bears false witness is to be punished as for the crime to which he gave the false witness (Deuteronomy 19:16-21).

When Christians fail to *"receive one another as Christ also received us"* (Romans 15:7), they set each other up as "competitors." When this happens, we fail to accept each others' differences. We fail to recognize that our differences can complement one another and that God has, for that very reason, given us to each other – so *together* we can be better than we would be without each other. Instead, we want others to be and act like we do. When they don't, we perceive them as doing something wrong and begin to gossip about them. Sometimes a simple difference in personality or preference will cause a Christian to speak evil of another person. Often the one being slandered doesn't know it – but he/she is entrapped because others in the church will often treat them coldly, having believed the false accusations about them. The one slandered often can't understand what they are doing wrong and why certain people don't seem friendly to them. Our service to each other and to the Lord is greatly weakened – and we grieve the Holy Spirit. *"And do not grieve the Holy Spirit of God, with whom you were sealed for the day of redemption. Get rid of all bitterness, rage and anger, brawling and slander, along with every form of malice."* Ephesians 4:30-31.

So does the Church have law enforcement officers? You might be surprised to find out who they are. Check out Romans 15:14 and Colossians 3:16.

WOLVES IN SHEEP'S CLOTHING

Christians struggle with maintaining peace and unity. What are the causes of division within the Body of Christ? Jesus said that in the last days the love of many would grow cold because iniquity will abound. I've sensed this coldness growing toward God, His work, and between brothers and sisters in Christ. Unsuspecting, unprepared Christians, who should be making disciples, are licking their wounds and wandering around looking for their perception of a real New Testament home church – only to be disillusioned again and again! Satan and his demons come as "angels of light" – messengers of truth – that appeal to man's weaknesses and lusts. They ambush otherwise sincere Christians by the attraction of position, prosperity, power, popularity, potential, and prestige. **These people then become like "wolves in sheep's clothing" to other Christians.** But Jesus said, *"... whosoever will save his life will lose it: and whosoever will lose his life for my sake shall find it."* (Matthew 16:25). He also said, *"Greater love hath no man than this, that a man lay down his life for his friends."* (John 15:13).

One of my books, ***Ambushed***, is written with the hope of changing the course of "shifting saints" from a desperate search for the right church to the passionate pursuit of making disciples. It's also written to help Christians understand important truths about living and leading in Christ's likeness and avoiding the enemy's snares – to escape the ambush and entrapment caused by the unseen powers of darkness. Our Lord never intended that His Church helplessly stand idle while Christians are needlessly persecuted from within. Members of the Church must stop hurting one another. We can no longer just pass by our wounded brothers and sisters who have been ambushed along the Jericho Road!

Have you ever met Evy Envy? Have you ever been Evy Envy? ***Evie Envy*** *was a member of the ladies group at her church. Clear Lee Sincere was the leader. Evie Envy was jealous of Clear and had influence with the pastor's wife. She used this influence to get things done the way she wanted in the group. She took away some of the special heart-to-heart ministries that Clear Lee Sincere had instituted and also made the meetings much less nurturing than before. As a result, attendance became more forced than spontaneous. Clear Lee was hurt and suffered in silence through the rest of her term in office. She refused to run for leadership the following year and Evie Envy became the new leader. Eventually the group dwindled and was abandoned.*

Young's Compact Bible Dictionary says that envy is similar to strife (i.e. conflict), schisms (i.e. divisions), and jealousy. Envy is deep in man's heart (Mark 7:22). It is in the list of the works of the flesh (Galatians 5: 20-21). It shows up in earthly "wisdom" (James 3:14-15). It is described in verse 15 as being "devilish". True love does not envy. (1 Corinthians 13: 4). Rachael was jealous of Leah's ability to bear children (Genesis 30:1).

Whenever we allow ourselves to envy one another, instead of perceiving brothers and sisters in Christ as "friends", we see them as our "competitors." We envy each other over our spouses, children, homes, education, financial security, and material possessions. We even envy one another about our Christian ministries – especially when we see someone getting more visibility and recognition than we from our leaders.

When this happens, we've built spiritual walls instead of bridges between us. The flow of encouragement, admonishment, and bearing one another's burdens is hindered. We may allow people to minister to us outwardly, but inwardly we don't receive these brethren as "gifts of God" to us. We inwardly hope they might fail in some way so we can feel better about our own lives and what we possess.

When envy occurs between a church leader (e.g. the pastor) and a church member who is gifted in his ministry, both of them become entrapped, discouraged, and less effective.

Evy Envy is just one of many "wolves in sheep's clothing." Let's not play into the devil's game plan for Christians: *"If you keep on biting and devouring each other, watch out or you will be destroyed by each other."* Galatians 5: 15

"WOUNDED IN THE HOUSE OF MY FRIENDS"

The Holy Spirit, speaking through Zechariah, spoke about the coming of Christ. He said, *"And I will pour upon the house of David, and upon the inhabitants of Jerusalem, the spirit of grace and of supplications: and they shall look upon me whom they have pierced, and they shall mourn for him , as one who mourns for his only son..."* Zechariah 12:10. *"And one shall say unto him, What are these wounds in your hands? Then he shall answer, Those with which I was wounded in the house of my friends."* Zechariah 13:6.

Jesus warned us that in this world we would be persecuted. See John 15:20. As He was persecuted in the house of His friends, we also will be persecuted for righteousness sake – often in our own churches. James 4:6 -10 NIV gives us guidance that, if followed by Christians, would prevent us from ambushing one another. In verse 6 we read, *"...God resists the proud but gives grace to the humble."* Let's stop right there for a moment. This says that we need to humble ourselves before God and confess our guilt before Him. We need to confess our sins.

We Christians need to agree with God that we have wronged our brothers and sisters. Our bitterness, lack of forgiveness, envy, betrayal, pride, immorality, slander, anger, and stealing (especially time and energy) against our brethren in Christ has wronged not only them but disappointed, shamed, and driven nails afresh into our Savior's old wounds! We need to repent over our sins toward the pastor God has given us – our laziness and gossip, our power-plays, lack of respect, submission, and obedience, our unbelief and over-bearing demands. Pastors need to confess their sins against their people – the patronizing, pushing, their insecurity and competitiveness, their false promises, and twisting Scripture to manipulate them.

We must not only admit our wrongs, but be willing to turn from them and surrender to God's transforming power (Romans 12:1-2). ***We all must admit that we have enjoyed being "saved" by our Savior but have fallen short of truly listening to Him as our Lord!*** We must daily confess our sins in order to stay close to Him and grow spiritually. He is faithful and just to forgive us when we truly repent and confess our sins (1 John 1:9).

James 4: 7-10 NIV continues, *"Submit yourselves, then, to God. Resist the devil and he will flee from you. Come near to God and he will come near to you. Wash your hands, you sinners, and purify your hearts, you double-minded. Grieve, mourn and wail. Change your laughter to mourning and your joy to gloom. Humble yourselves before the Lord, and he will lift you up."* James continues in verses 13-15, *"Now listen, you who say, 'Today or tomorrow we will go to this or that city, spend a year there, carry on business and make money.' Why, you do not even know what will happen tomorrow. What is your life? You are a mist that appears for a little while and then vanishes. Instead, you ought to say, 'If it is the Lord's will, we will live and do this or that.'"*

I believe that we allow the devil to ambush us or to use us to ambush others because we don't truly want to OR are ignorant of how to "submit ourselves and come near to God." Light dispels darkness. Christians need to embrace the "light" – the knowledge of Christ.

LIVE BY FAITH – NOT BY FLESH. Speaking of Jesus Christ, the Apostle John said, *"In him was life, and that life was the light of men. The light shines in the darkness, but the darkness has not overpowered it."* (NIV note a). John further says, *"If we claim to have fellowship with him yet walk in the darkness, we lie and do not put the truth into practice. But if we walk in the light, as he is in the light, we have fellowship with one another, and the blood of Jesus, his Son, purifies us from every sin."* (1 John 1:6-7 NIV).

We need to walk where Jesus walks – in the light with understanding. Then we will have "fellowship" with each other – we will share life with each other the way God intended. We will accept one another the way we are till God shapes us into what He wants us to be.

We need to stop *living by flesh* and start *living by faith*. We need to stop living as "carnal Christians", allowing our natural man and his values to dominate and drive our lives. That's how the devil gets a foothold in our lives and ambushes us and our brothers and sisters in Christ. In addition, when the flesh dominates, the unsaved see "self" in us (and in our church) instead of seeing Christ – as the Lord intended.

Please take seriously our Lord's warning to us about what will happen in the last days, *"And because iniquity shall abound, the love of many shall wax cold"* (Matthew 24:12). Whose love? It's not the world's love that Christ spoke about because the world's love has always been cold. No, it's the love of those in the Body of Christ – our love! As Christians hurt each other, their love for God and each other will grow cold! Remember, Jesus also said, *"Not everyone that says to me, Lord, Lord, shall enter into the kingdom of heaven; but he that does the will of my father who is in heaven...And then will I profess unto them, depart from me, you that work iniquity"* (Matthew 7:21-23).

NEVER, NEVER, NEVER GIVE UP!

We need to stop playing into the devil's plan for Christians to destroy one another (Galatians 5:15) – which hinders and can eventually stop the spread of the gospel. It's as if a spear is (once again) being thrust into the Body of Christ! We need to sincerely repent of ambushing others. If we've been on the receiving end, we need to repent of not extending forgiveness. We need to decide TODAY to stop living by flesh and begin wholeheartedly living by faith – to take the spiritual vitamins that will transform us, with the daily help of the Holy Spirit, into the Christlike person He wants us to become. Let's fix our spiritual eyes upon Christ's priorities, character qualities, and behaviors with vigor, and ask our Father to make us like Him!

Let's take seriously the Apostle Paul's exhortation and warning to the Ephesians, *"You were taught, with regard to your former way of life, to put off your old self, which is being corrupted by its deceitful desires; to be made new in the attitude of your minds; and to put on the new self, created to be like God with true righteousness and holiness...put off falsehood and speak truthfully...In your anger do not sin...do not give the devil a foothold...steal no longer...Do not let any unwholesome talk come out of your mouths, but only what is helpful for building others up...Get rid of all bitterness, rage and anger, brawling and slander, along with every form of malice.*

Be kind and compassionate to one another, forgiving each other, just as in Christ God forgave you. Be imitators of God, therefore, as dearly loved children and live a life of love, just as Christ loved us and gave himself up for us...But among you there must not be even a hint of sexual immorality, or any kind of impurity, or of greed, because these are improper for God's holy people...For of this you can be sure: No immoral, impure, or greedy person...has any inheritance in the kingdom of Christ and of God." Ephesians 4:22 – 5:5.

NEVER GIVE UP! There may be times when you'll be discouraged and feel "beat up" from being persecuted and ambushed in your walk with the Lord. But you must never give up! Never, never, never give up! In his book, ***The Fight***, John White writes, "It is the man or woman who gets up and fights again that is the true warrior…Strengthen yourself with a powerful draught of the wine of Romans 8:1-4. Then get back into the fight before your muscles get stiff!"

"What's required is dogged endurance, keeping at the task of obedience through the ebbs and flows, ups and downs, victories and losses in life. It is trying again, while knowing that God is working in you to accomplish His purposes. Philippians 1:6; 2:13. It is persistently pursuing God's will for your life till you stand before Him and your work is done. God is wonderfully persistent too. He will never, never, never give up on you!" (David H. Roper, OUR DAILY BREAD, November 2001, p. 28). *"...be content with what you have, because God has said, 'Never will I leave you; never will I forsake you.' So we say with confidence, 'The Lord is my helper; I will not be afraid. What can man do to me?'"* Hebrews 13:5, 6.

The Apostle Paul told the Thessalonians, *"...we boast about your perseverance and faith in all the persecutions and trials you are enduring."* 2 Thessalonians 1:4. *"May the Lord direct your hearts into God's love and Christ's perseverance."* 2 Thessalonians 3:5. *"And as for you, brothers, **never tire of doing what is right**."* 2 Thessalonians 3:13.

The Lord was encouraging and warning the seven churches (and us) in Revelation 2 & 3. He was giving them (and us) time to better prepare and be ready for His return. The Lord had four main messages for those seven churches:

Before He gave each church His judgment about them, He always gave them a picture of Himself. It was the portrait they needed for their specific circumstances. He was telling them (and us) to always keep who He is in the center of our hearts and minds. For example, to the Philadelphia church He introduced Himself as, *"...he that is holy, he that is true, he that hath the key of David, he that openeth and no man shutteth; and shutteth and no man openeth..."* Revelation 3:7.

He told every church that He knew their works. This can be reassuring but for some of us it should at times be disconcerting too! The Lord knows us inside and out. He knows when we get off track and run in wrong directions – how we ambush one another with anger, jealousy, deceit, immorality, slander, unforgiveness, pride, stealing, and betrayal.

He told four of the seven churches to repent. *"If we confess our sins, he is faithful and just to forgive us our sins, and to cleanse us from all unrighteousness."* 1 John 1:9. Let's resolve to change the wrong beliefs, attitudes, and behaviors we see in ourselves. Let's commit to the Lord that we will take our stand against such things in the Church.

He told all the churches to overcome. How do we overcome? God gave Joshua the answer as he took charge of God's people, *"There shall not any man be able to stand before thee all the days of thy life: as I was with Moses, so I will be with thee; I will not fail thee, nor forsake thee. Be strong and of good courage: for unto this people shalt thou divide for an inheritance the land...Only be thou strong and courageous...Be strong and of good courage; be not afraid, neither be thou dismayed: for the Lord thy God is with thee whithersoever thou goest."* Joshua 1: 5-9. Remember that Jesus also told us that *He would never leave nor forsake us*. Hebrews 13:5. The Apostle Paul added that we could do all things *through Christ who strengthens us*. Philippians 4:13.

With the Holy Spirit in us, we can (***and must***) overcome, and by unity with our brothers and sisters in Christ witness to a dying world that Jesus Christ is the Way to eternal life. Let's entrust ourselves to God's ultimate, always loving purposes. By doing that, we can know that we are really completing the work that our heavenly Father gave us to do. That will be like nourishment for our soul to never give up until we cross the finish line of faith – true warriors and more than conquerors!

Chapter 5

Fire in the Soul For Heaven

Echoes from Heaven[6]

Far away among the angels,
In the sweet celestial bow'rs,
Start the songs whose echoes gladden
As they greet this world of ours.

How they stir the soul with rapture!
How they thrill the chords of love!
How they wake the songs of praises,
Floating up to worlds above!

Far away in worlds of glory,
We can hear the music sweet,
Where the streams of life are flowing
All along the golden street.

Far away in fields of glory
We shall meet, and God adore;
And the sweet redemption story
We shall sing forevermore.

Refrain:
Hear the echoes filled with glory,
From the bright angelic throng;
Oh, the pure seraphic music
Finds an echo in our song,
While it gently rolls along.

---

[6] Barney E. Warren, *pub.* 1911

HEAVEN SCENT – AND OTHER THINGS ABOUT OUR FUTURE HOME

When Jesus gave the Apostle John a revelation of our future, John saw the 24 elders fall down before Christ in heaven, each one having a harp and golden bowls full of incense (or odors), which are the prayers of the saints. Revelation 5: 8. So we know heaven is full of a sweet smelling scent from our prayers. What else can we know about heaven?

We know it is called "Father's house" where Jesus is preparing a place for us to be where He is – just like a Jewish bridegroom who goes to his father's house to add on a room for he and his future bride. When the father approves, the groom then goes to get his bride and bring her home. John 14: 1-3. And we know that Jesus is coming back to take us (rapture us) home to be with Him forever. 1 Thessalonians 4: 16-17. At the same time Jesus is preparing a place for us, John 14:23 tells us that we are to prepare a place (i.e. Father's house) within ourselves for the Holy Spirit by obeying God's Word. We are also told that the Kingdom of God is within us – it is righteousness, peace, and joy in the Holy Ghost. And that since Christ ascended to be at the Father's right hand, we too are now there in Christ. Therefore, we can sense heaven right inside us now, while Christ prepares our real future eternal dwelling. Luke 17: 21; Romans 14: 17; Colossians 3: 1.

When Jesus returns to rapture his saints, we know that in a twinkling of an eye those who have died and gone to heaven and those still alive will receive immortal, incorruptible bodies – like the one Jesus had when He resurrected. *"...we know that, when he appears, we shall be like him..."* 1 Corinthians 15: 51-52; 1 John 3: 2. Not only will we have bodies that cannot die, but we will have the radiance – the bright light around us – like when Jesus was transfigured before His disciples. See Luke 9:29. Daniel 12: 3 says, *"Those who are wise will shine like the brightness of the heavens, and those who lead many to righteousness, like the stars for ever and ever."* In our foreheads we will carry Christ's name: The Light of the World. Revelation 22: 4. It's interesting that the word for "transfigured" or "changed" in Luke 9: 29 is the same word translated "transformed" in Romans 12: 2, where we are urged to be transformed (within) by the renewing of our minds!

When we die in Christ, our souls and spirits go to be with the Lord immediately – like Jesus told the thief on the cross next to Him, *"I tell you the truth, today you will be with me in paradise."* Luke 23: 43. It's like God taking back His "breath of life" that He breathed into man's nostrils to make him a living being at Creation. Genesis 2: 7. Where do we wait in heaven to receive our immortal bodies? The Apostle John caught sight of those who were martyred for their faith during the Great Tribulation period, *"...I saw under the altar the souls of those who had been slain because of the word of God and the testimony they had maintained."* Revelation 6: 9. Could that be where we wait, or is that place for martyrs only? When Jesus told the story of Lazarus and the rich man (Luke 16: 19-31), He said that Lazarus *"was carried by the angels into Abraham's bosom."* Maybe that's the area of heaven in which we await our incorruptible bodies?

More likely, we are living in the heavenly city – the New Jerusalem, which later John sees descending from heaven. See Hebrews 11: 16; 12: 22; 13: 14. We learn from the story of Lazarus and the rich man that we will definitely be able to recognize one another – so there will be an immediate reunion of those who have gone to heaven before us! How do we get to heaven? Jesus said, ***"I am the way, and the truth, and the life. No one comes to the Father except through me."*** John 14: 6. There aren't "many paths" to heaven – Father's house is found only through trusting in Christ's death for our sins and His resurrection!

What will we do in heaven? We will all experience the Judgment Seat of Christ – *"that each one may receive what is due him for the things done while in the body, whether good or bad."* 2 Corinthians 5: 10. There will be both tears and great joy there. Tears because we will regret missing opportunities we were given to glorify Christ. And great joy when Christ's smile dries our tears and He says, *"Well done, good and faithful servant!"* This experience makes us ready for the marriage supper of the Lamb. Revelation 19: 6-9. After that, we will follow the Lord to fight one last time for righteousness at the Battle of Armageddon. Revelation 19: 11-21. What joy will fill our hearts when the Jews recognize Jesus as their Messiah! Zechariah 13: 6.

Then we rule & reign with Jesus for 1000 years – like His Parable of the Ten Minas, *"...Well done, my good servant his master replied. Because you have been trustworthy in a very small matter, take charge of ten cities."* Luke 19: 11-26. I believe that in heaven we will receive training to rule from the Master-Servant Himself. We'll also be able to share our experiences on earth with those who went to heaven before us. We'll learn from those God used to write His Word – Moses, the prophets and apostles. We'll learn how to travel using our new heavenly bodies; and about many more mysteries of the universe. I believe we'll be helping to build the New Jerusalem, whose foundation is built with every kind of precious stone – gems that represent Christ's redemptive work in the life of believers. See 1 Corinthians 3: 12 – 14; 1 Peter 1: 7; Revelation 21: 19-20.

And lest I forget, *"No eye has seen, no ear has heard, no mind has conceived what God has prepared for those who love him."* 1 Corinthians 2: 9. Words are inadequate to describe the One sitting on a magnificent throne, who is the Blessed Controller of all things, who had the appearance of jasper and carnelian, with a rainbow of emerald encircling the throne – the thunder and lightning from the throne – before the throne a sea of glass clear as crystal – Christ in all His glory - the living creatures that represent Christ our Life – the temple and angels – the scrolls containing records of everyone's conduct – the awesome light – the New

Jerusalem city! And we will see His face, and our minds will be stayed upon Him and be in perfect peace. Revelation 22: 4; Isaiah 26: 3.

HEAVEN – THE CITY WHOSE BUILDER AND MAKER IS GOD

Hebrews 11: 10 declares that Abraham *"waited for a city which has foundations, whose builder and maker is God."* Speaking of all those who died in the faith, Hebrews 11:16 says, *"Therefore God is not ashamed to be called their God, for He has prepared a city for them."* What city are these verses talking about? It's the heavenly city called "The New Jerusalem".

It's the place in heaven that Jesus is preparing for us to spend eternity. John 14: 1-3. It's the future home for all of God's people from where we will rule and reign with Him. One day, after Christ's 1000-year reign as King of kings on earth (Revelation 20: 6), when God creates a new heaven and new earth (Revelation 21: 1), this city will descend from heaven and it will light up the earth.

I like to call it "Honeymoon City" because God and we will dwell together and we shall see Him face to face forever. *"...the throne of God and of the Lamb shall be in it; and his servants shall serve him: And they shall see his face; and his name shall be in their foreheads. And there shall be no night there; and they need no candle, neither the light of the sun; for the Lord God giveth them light: and they shall reign for ever and ever."* Revelation 22: 3-5. It's "Honeymoon City" also because the angel who was showing it to John told him that this city was prepared as a bride (the Church) adorned for her husband (Christ). Revelation 21: 2.

My favorite name for it, however, is "Showcase City" because – like the winner of a race who runs the victory lap - God will have us on display for the whole universe to see the glorious and redemptive work of Christ. The crowds that once shouted for us to glorify "self" and follow the world, the flesh, and the devil, will be gone. In their place will be a "cloud of witnesses" throughout the universe who will constantly bask in the light of "Showcase City". They will shout the praises of God and His Christ as they are eternally reminded of God's awesome, magnificent victory!

How could a city be "adorned" to be a bride? And how could it be a showcase? Let's look at the New Jerusalem. The Church is housed there – all the born-again believers from all time. They adorn its streets. We shall be shining like the stars in the firmament. Daniel 12: 3. In a way, we'll be like the precious stones that form the foundation of the City. Revelation 21: 19-21. Precious stones that have been cut and shaped in the "heat" of this wondrous race of life our Father, through Christ, has given us to run by the power of the Holy Spirit.

The names of the twelve tribes of Israel, the descendants of those fore-runners Abraham, Isaac, and Jacob, are inscribed at each of the twelve entrance gates. Revelation 21: 12. And each of these gates were made of a ***single pearl*** (Revelation 21:21) – like "the pearl of great price" Jesus spoke of – which represents Christ Himself. The only way into the City is through Christ – the Entrance. *"...the kingdom of heaven is like unto a merchant man, seeking goodly pearls: Who, when he had found one pearl of great price, went and sold all that he had, and bought it."* Matthew 13:45-46.

The foundations of the City have the names of Christ's twelve Apostles inscribed there. Revelation 21: 14. And the streets are of purest gold like transparent glass (Revelation 21: 21) – gold that Peter said was the precious faith of believers when it was tried with fire. 1Peter 1: 7. Finally, this City has *"the glory of God: and her light was like unto a stone most precious, even like a jasper stone, clear as crystal."* Revelation 21:11. It was like a great glass case that contained the precious jewels of the Lord (His people shining like stars) being displayed for the entire universe for ever and ever as a final victory lap of those who ran the race of life God's way.

Some might ask, "Who in the universe will be there to see this great display – the Bride of the Lamb – the City of God's precious love?" Who will be cheering the Victor and victors? We know that the angels will be there, but who else? *"And the nations of them which are saved shall walk in the light of it: and the kings of the earth do bring their glory and honor into it. And the gates of it shall not be shut at all by day: for there shall be no night there. And they shall bring the glory and honor of the nations into it."* Revelation 21:24-26. There will be surviving nations who did not fall for the deceit of Satan after he was loosed from his thousand-year imprisonment! These nations will be those we will *"rule and reign for ever and ever"*. Revelation 22: 5.

Those who do fall for the devil's deceit, who rebel against Christ, as well as all unbelievers from the beginning of time will be cast into the lake of fire, which is eternal death. Revelation 21: 15. Life will then proceed as God originally intended for His creation to live.

The City will be about 1400 miles high, long, and wide. It will have a river flowing through its center, from top to bottom. It will come from the *"throne of God and of the Lamb."* And on either side of the river there will be the tree of life, which will bear twelve different fruits – a different one every month. The leaves of this tree *"were for the healing of the nations."* Revelation 22:1-2. The leaves of the tree of life will "heal" the survivors of the disaster caused by the rebellion against Christ. God acted with great love when He sent Adam and Eve out of the garden so they could not eat of the tree of life – because they would have lived forever in sin – and us too! Genesis 3: 22. God killed an animal to provide clothing to cover the nakedness of Adam and Eve. Later on, He would provide the blood of the Lamb to cover our sins. In Revelation 22: 13, Jesus says, *"I am the Alpha and Omega, the beginning and the end, the first and the last."*

In the New Jerusalem, people eat from the tree of life freely. People live as God intended from the beginning with no more curse from sin. Revelation 22: 3. God's home is with men and He shall wipe away all tears from their eyes. There shall be no more death, nor sorrow, nor crying, nor shall there be any more pain. The former things will all pass away and God will make everything new. Revelation 21: 4-5.

HEAVEN – ENTRANCE REQUIREMENTS & OUR PURPOSE HERE ON EARTH

Getting into heaven happens only through Jesus Christ. Remember, He is the "Pearly Gate" into the New Jerusalem! So it involves the acceptance by faith of the following truths:

- *"There is none righteous, no, not one."* (Romans 3:10). *"All we like sheep have gone astray; we have turned every one to his own way..."* (Isaiah 53:6). All our righteousness (i.e. "right living") is as filthy rags to God, who is pure holiness. (Isaiah 64:6)
- *"For all have sinned and come short of the glory of God."* (Romans 3:23)
- *"Your iniquities (i.e. sins) have separated between you and your God, and your sins have hid his face from you..."* (Isaiah 59:2)
- *"Wherefore, as by one man (i.e. Adam) sin entered into the world, and death by sin; and so death passed upon all men, for that all have sinned."* (Romans 5:12)

But, there is a solution…

- *"But God commends his love toward us, in that, while we were yet sinners Christ died for us."* (Romans 5:8)
- *"For there is one God, and one mediator between God and men, the man Christ Jesus; who gave himself a ransom for all..."* (1Timothy 2:5-6)
- *"For the wages of sin is death; but the gift of God is eternal life through Jesus Christ our Lord."* (Romans 6:23)
- *"Ye were... redeemed with the precious blood of Christ, as of a lamb without blemish and without spot."* (1Peter 1:18-19)

- *"For whosoever shall call upon the name of the Lord shall be saved."* (Romans 10:13)
- *"If thou shalt confess with thy mouth the Lord Jesus and shalt believe in thine heart that God hath raised him from the dead, thou shalt be saved."* (Romans 10:9)
- *"For with the heart man believeth unto righteousness; and with the mouth confession is made unto salvation... Whosoever believeth on him shall not be ashamed."* (Romans 10: 10-11)

When we accept these truths and sincerely ask Jesus to be our Savior and Lord, we are "receiving Jesus" and are "born-again"- literally "born from above". John 1: 10-13 says that Jesus came unto his own and his own received him not. But to all those who received him, he gave them the power to become children of God – even those who believe in His name – who were born not of blood, nor the will of man, *but born of God* (i.e. born from above or born-again). We enter the family of God and (just like blood is common in earthly family members) God sends His Holy Spirit to take up residence in all believers (i.e. members of God's spiritual family).

We are "Christians" <u>only</u> when we have received Christ and are born-again. As Christians, our purpose on earth is to be a reflection of Christ – Christ beings. It's a life-long process of surrendering as living sacrifices, trusting and obeying God, so He can transform us from the inside – especially the way we think and act - into the image of His dear Son. Romans 12: 1-2. Paul summarized our purpose here this way, *"I consider everything a loss compared to the surpassing greatness of knowing Christ Jesus my Lord, for whose sake I have lost all things...that I might gain Christ...I want to know Christ and the power of his resurrection and the fellowship of sharing in his sufferings, becoming like him...Forgetting what is behind and straining toward what is ahead, I press on toward the goal to win the prize for which God has called me heavenward in Christ Jesus."* Philippians 3: 8-14.

While we live and work here, our purpose is to develop a deeper, closer relationship (i.e. walk) with Jesus Christ. He must always be our First Love! As we do, we will produce the fruit of our salvation out to others – love, joy, peace, patience, kindness, goodness, faithfulness, gentleness and self-control. To energize and direct our walk to maturity in Christ, God has given us a diet of spiritual vitamins to take regularly and keep in balance:

Vitamin A – **A**sk – Prayer (Ephesians 6: 18)
Vitamin B – **B**ible – Study God's Word (2 Timothy 2: 15)
Vitamin C – **C**omfort – Comfort others with the same comfort we've received from God during our own trials and suffering (2 Corinthians 1: 4-5)
Vitamin D – **D**o – Getting involved in some ministry to help others (Matthew 25: 14-30)
Vitamin E – **E**xalt – Worship the Lord with our heart, mind, and strength (Psalm 100: 4)
Vitamin K – **K**oinonia (Greek word) – Fellowship with other believers (Acts 2: 42-47)

Living the real Christian life is like riding a bicycle. There are trials and suffering for us all while we live here on earth – but sometimes we cause our own problems and make the ride "bumpy" for several reasons:

- The spokes of the wheel (the spiritual vitamins) keep our Christian life (the rim of the wheel) connected to Christ (the hub of the wheel). The spokes need to be kept in balance – some of us love to worship regularly - but only study the Word when necessary. Some love to study but sharing their life in fellowship is too "close". Different size spokes cause a rough ride.

- Christ must be in the center of our lives – the "hub" of the wheel. We often put ourselves back in that place.

- **As the spokes get longer, pumping the bike to go forward farther is easier because the wheel is bigger. If the spokes**

are short, however, we have to pump hard to cover just a short distance because the wheel is small.

As we run the race of life God's way, we need to make the course of our lives a journey that we savor. Knowing God and being like Christ is our goal. Prayer, Word Study, Worship, Fellowship, Service, and Trials/Suffering are the highways where we will find our Divine Running Partner and Coach, Jesus Christ. They are the pathways He has carved with His own footprints, the exercise gear to strengthen and shape us, the guideposts to mark off the course, and the track shoes to securely grip the grains of shifting sand on the race track of our lives. *"My soul longeth, yea, even fainteth for the courts of the Lord: my heart and my flesh crieth out for the living God...Blessed is the man whose strength is in thee; in whose heart are the highways to Zion."* (R.V.) (Psalm 84:2, 5)

Working for God on earth doesn't pay much, but His retirement plan is out of this world!

HEAVEN - JUDGMENT DAY FOR CHRISTIANS

We Christians "*must all appear before the judgment seat of Christ.*" 2 Corinthians 5: 10. Have you ever wondered how we who have been serving Christ will be judged? The Church needs to know how we'll be measured so we can live now with a view toward eternity, avoid destructive confrontation, and fulfill God's plan for our lives. Here's a vision (a dream) I received concerning what this Judgment Seat of Christ might be all about…

I was launched into a heavenly realm where I stood with ten thousand times ten thousand and thousands of thousands. They were from *every kindred, tongue, people, and nation.* In the midst of these vast numbers of people stood a Judgment Seat and there in all His glory was Christ, Himself. All the people (including me) praised Him and the sound of our cheers was deafening.

Then something very strange happened. Jesus looked at me. It seemed that the Lord's eye caught the eye of everyone at the same time. It was probably like what happened to Peter – after he had denied the Lord three times – when Jesus looked at him. Luke 22: 61. The noise of the crowd seemed to hush and I could only see Christ's eye. The Lord's look only lasted a moment, but it seemed like a lifetime. I'd experienced being heart-to-heart with the Lord, but now we were eye-to-eye.

I was lifted to spiritual heights unknown to me. I saw a stability - surpassing the tallest of earth's mountains; a strength – surpassing the combined force of the wind and ocean during a violent storm; a purity - surpassing the smallest of infants; a peace - surpassing the most tranquil waters; a deep, genuine care and concern – surpassing a mother's love for her nursing child; a joy - surpassing a father who receives back his rebellious son; and, a hope - surpassing the runner about to pass the finish line first.

With that look, the Lord searched to see His own image in me. But I began to see myself reflected back to me - certain opportunities I had missed to share the Gospel or to emulate Christ – times when I worked for Christ in my own strength instead of His. Tears flowed over my face as I viewed these things – because I saw them being burned up like wood, hay, and stubble. 1 Corinthians 3:11-15.

Then my eyes, as if controlled by a source outside myself, viewed more and more of the Lord's face – not just His eye. When I caught a glimpse of His mouth, the Lord began to smile with such warmth that my tears were dried up instantly and I began to feel a certain glow about me. Then the Lord called me by a new name that He said came from surrendering my "self" life to serve Jesus and others. Romans 12: 1- 2.

Then the Lord set me at the bottom of an inverted pyramid with rejoicing people whom I knew during my lifetime arranged along the sides and top of the pyramid. The Lord then began to tell me what happened to them. The Lord began, "Do you remember this lady who was on the bus, who was almost ready to deny My existence? You ran after her, witnessed to her, and she received Me there in the parking lot. Do you remember? She became a Sunday school teacher and led many children to accept me also." And as He spoke, those children – that I'd never met - were added to the pyramid. "Remember this young man in your singles group who became a pastor? He got a church in the inner city and made disciples who also went on to bring My gospel to many others." When He said that, more people that I'd never met were added and the pyramid got even bigger. The Lord said, "Do you remember these sixty people who accepted Me during the lay witness mission that you led? They each brought one more to me." And more people were added to the pyramid.

The Lord continued to tell me about the young soldier, who I helped find his way back to Christ; the lesbian, who accepted Him and became a Sunday school teacher; all the members of my Sunday school classes, workshops, and seminars. There were many that I touched but was unaware of – some were children of parents I helped stay together – others were people I prayed for unceasingly, not knowing any of the results.

As I looked at everyone in the pyramid above me, I remembered what the Apostle Paul had told the Thessalonians, *"For what is our hope, our joy, or the crown in which we will glory in the presence of our Lord Jesus Christ when he comes? Is it not you? Indeed, you are our glory and joy."* 1 Thessalonians 2:19-20. I realized that the Lord had created a crown of rejoicing people all around me!

When the Lord finished speaking with me, I noticed that I was not at the very bottom of this crown. Esther, the woman who led me to Christ, was under me. I was only a small part of her crown. Under her was another, and another further down, and that continued further and further downward. At the very bottom of the pyramid, with an uncountable number in the crown, was Christ. He had the greatest and largest crown! He said, "Do you remember when I told you that if you would be the greatest in My kingdom, you should be the servant of all? I told you, *"Whosoever desires to be first among you, let him be your slave – just as the Son of Man did not come to be served but to serve, and to give his life a ransom for many."* Matthew 20: 27-28.

I realized that Jesus was First and Last – that He was the Source as well as the Finish Line of my faith. But there was something even below Christ. I realized, after a while of straining to see, that at the very bottom of the crown was the image of a broken heart – it was the Father's broken heart. But His heart was healed!

Suddenly, I felt another crown upon my head and the Lord said, "Behold your hope, and joy, and crown of rejoicing. Are not these people, to whom you ministered, who are now in My presence, your hope, joy, and crown?" Then without delay I cast my crown at the Lord's feet and these words fell effortlessly from my lips,

"You alone are worthy, O Lord, to receive the glory and honor and power." Revelation 4: 10-11. Immediately the space around me became brilliant with light. And I remembered what Daniel had said, *"They that turn many to righteousness shall shine as the stars for ever and ever."* See Daniel 12:3.

When I awoke, I fell to my knees and rededicated my life to Christ. I asked forgiveness for not using every opportunity the Lord had given me to share Christ with others. I asked forgiveness for the times I "lived by flesh" rather than living by faith and trust in Christ. I wanted more than ever before to tell people about Him – His stability, strength, purity, love, joy, peace, and hope – to tell Christians about their appointment with Him at the Judgment Seat.

Chapter 6

Keep the Flame of God's Word Burning Brightly

Wonderful Words of Life[7]

Sing them over again to me, wonderful words of life,
Let me more of their beauty see, wonderful words of life;
Words of life and beauty teach me faith and duty.

Christ, the Blessèd One, gives to all wonderful words of life;
Sinner, list to the loving call, wonderful words of life;
All so freely given, wooing us to heaven.

Sweetly echo the Gospel call, wonderful words of life;
Offer pardon and peace to all, wonderful words of life;
Jesus, only Savior, sanctify us forever.

Refrain
Beautiful words, wonderful words, wonderful words of life,
Beautiful words, wonderful words, wonderful words of life.

[7] Philip P. Bliss, 1874

THE HOUR OF POWER

I don't care about when it happens. It can be before Sunday morning service, after service, or between services. I don't care what you call it. It can be "Sunday School", "Bible Study", "Church School", or the "Christian Education Hour." Whatever it's called, <u>it should be the most important hour of the week for the Christian</u>. If your weak "flesh", or the "world", or the devil robs that from you and your family, they will also have their way in other areas of your life that go unprotected by the knowledge of God's Word.

Some say, "The sermon is enough." Sermons, however, are primarily for *inspiration*. Sunday School is primarily for *education* in God's Word. There is the gift of preaching – that's not the gift of teaching. Some say, "That's the only day I get to sleep late." But the Scripture says, *"Love not sleep, lest thou come to poverty; open thine eyes, and thou shalt be satisfied with bread."* Proverbs 20:13. This relates to providing for your family – not just "poverty" of pocketbook, but also "poverty" of soul. Not just "bread" to feed the stomach, but also the "Bread of Life" to feed the mind, heart, and spirit.

Paul's last words to Timothy included, *"Study to show thyself approved unto God, a workman that needeth not to be ashamed, rightly dividing the word of truth."* 2 Timothy 2:15. *"...and how from infancy you have known the holy Scriptures which are able to make you wise for salvation through faith in Christ Jesus. All Scripture is God-breathed and is useful for teaching, rebuking, correcting and training in righteousness, so that the man of God may be thoroughly equipped for every good work."* 2 Timothy 3:15-17 NIV. Jesus, our Lord and Teacher, taught us, *"Come to me, all you that are weary and burdened, and I will give you rest. Take my yoke upon you and* ***learn of me****...*" Matthew 11:28NIV.

Here's how God got me started teaching adults about 28 years ago – how He worked with this still rather stubborn Christian: I worked for the Army in Germany and made several trips to the U.S. every year. Once on the return trip, I had two seats to myself and was so grateful to be able to stretch out. The stewardess was about to close the door, when another man jumped on the plane. His seat was next to me. And soon we were sharing our Christian testimonies. He was a missionary to the soldiers, and we shared each other's phone numbers and addresses. One day, I got a call from a sailor who had been at the missionary's meetings. He had told the sailor that he was sure I would love to host a Bible study for him and his friends.

This Bible study and fellowship proved to last two years and showed me that the Lord was faithful and could use me in a teaching ministry – something that God would use throughout my walk. People were saved through this Bible study. One lesbian in the Army, who kept very quiet for many of the Bible study meetings, eventually accepted Jesus as her Savior and Lord. Her life was transformed. She married and later had children and was teaching Bible studies herself. This home Bible study resulted in my beginning to teach Sunday School in our church and also co-leading a group of one hundred Christians who met on Sunday night for worship and prayer time. Our Bible study group learned how to care for and be accountable to one another – something that Sunday School provides as well. For example, when one of the guys had missed our meeting and also didn't show up for duty, the others went and found him "hung over" in his quarters. They nursed him with "coffee and prayer" back to his job and our Bible study.

Here are some other thoughts from a Sunday School teacher...

With my teaching responsibility comes accountability to the Lord and my fellow Christians to "walk the talk". Fourteen years ago, when my first wife left me for another man (after 25 years) I thought my walk with the Lord before the brethren (and especially my Sunday School class) was irrevocably tarnished for ever. I began really examining my life. And though I felt that I had been faithful to Him, **I realized that I was fitting God into my schedule instead of making Him first.** I studied the Word only to prepare my Sunday School lesson. I prayed and worshipped Him only in my car on the way to work. **So I began putting Him first and making time to study the Word**, pray and worship Him. I've read the Bible through every year since then. Putting Him first is something I suggest to those who want to "sleep in" and miss Sunday School. By the way, my class began to see a new fervor, focus, and faithfulness that weren't there before – His strength not mine!

As a teacher, I appreciate opportunities to learn from others. I don't always agree with everything that I hear, but I look for the small jewels – the treasures from *"His riches in glory by Christ Jesus"*. Aside from the actual experience of teaching and being energized by the Holy Spirit, those jewels become most precious to my soul. If we maintain a "new wineskin heart", the Lord is able to "stretch us" with new truth from His Word. See Luke 5: 36-39. Something that really bothers me as a teacher is when I hear the brethren sing words during worship time with great emotion that their actions show me they don't really believe. They sing that they love God – and that He is all in all - but don't attend Sunday School to learn of Him and by Him. They sing, "I surrender all" but don't surrender an extra hour on Sunday morning to get "equipped for every good work."

Go to Sunday School and experience what David said, *"How sweet are thy words to my taste! yea sweeter than honey to my mouth." Psalm 119:103. "O taste and see that the Lord is good..." Psalm 34:8.*

LEARNING TO STAND - CHRISTIAN EDUCATORS SHOW US HOW

My newest grandson, Jimmy "the Goo", is about 18 months old. He's been walking for a couple of months now, but I remember how much he struggled to stand on his feet. He couldn't get his balance for a long time and needed someone to hold his hands. That reminded me of what we must do as Christian educators and leaders – we need to provide a good foundation (i.e. some basic understanding) to help Christians take their stand for Christ with balance and good perspective. This is necessary if they are to walk intimately with God and emulate Christ. Here are some things I believe are basic…

First, we need to understand that we are all "works in progress", and learn to practice the things that will help us grow in our relationship with the Lord – make these our regular habits. I like to call them our spiritual vitamins. They will help reduce the "flesh" and allow God to form His Son in us. They help make us "perfectly weak" like Abraham needed to be so God could form Isaac in his union with Sarah. God told him, *"Walk before me and be thou perfect."* Genesis 17:1. The spiritual vitamins should be "taken" in large, equal doses with gallons of gratitude to the Lord.

VITAMIN A = ASK (i.e. prayer). See Ephesians 6:18. We should pray with our families or find prayer partners. **VITAMIN B = BIBLE** (i.e. study the Word of God). See 2 Timothy 2:15. **VITAMIN C = COMFORT** (i.e. when we see others going through suffering and trials, comfort them with the comfort we've received from the Lord when we suffered). See 2 Corinthians 1:4. **VITAMIN D = DO** (i.e. get involved in some service for the Lord that helps others). See Matthew 25:14-30. **VITAMIN E = EXALT** (i.e. worship the Lord with all our heart). See Psalms

100:4. **VITAMIN K = KOININIA** (i.e. Greek word that means fellowship with those the Lord has set us with in the Body). See Acts 2: 42-47.

Next, Christian educators and leaders need to teach us to embrace the priorities and character qualities (i.e. values) that the Lord gave us to "see" Him better. Hebrews 12: 2 tells us to run the Christian race "*looking unto Jesus, the Author and Finisher of our faith.*" These values are found in His cross and are essential for walking in step with the Lord…

SERVING OTHERS. Romans 12: 1-2 reminds us to surrender to God (the Potter) so He can shape us for service. This is the self-sacrifice of the cross – *"For God so loved the world that He gave His only begotten Son, that whosoever believes in Him should not perish but have everlasting life."* John 3:16

HEART-TO-HEART. This means allowing others to know us and taking the time to get to know others in the church. This is the love of the cross – *"But God demonstrates His own love for us in this: While we were still sinners, Christ died for us."* Romans 5:8.

WISDOM FROM ABOVE. *"The wisdom that comes from heaven is first of all* ***pure****; then peace-loving, considerate, submissive, full of mercy and good fruit, impartial and sincere."* James 3:17. This is the holiness of the cross - *"God made Him who had no sin to be sin for us, so that in Him we might become the righteousness of God."* 2 Corinthians 5:21.

PULL-DON'T PUSH. We don't use, abuse, or manipulate others to make them do what we want. Instead, like Christ, we draw them to us. This is the humility and obedience of the cross. *"And being found in appearance as a man, He humbled Himself and became obedient to death – even the death of the cross."* Philippians 2:8.

When we take our spiritual vitamins and embrace His values, over time we gain the balance to stand. Then we can walk in His footsteps and produce in a natural way the behaviors of Christ. Here are some that I consider very important…

LISTEN TO WHAT OTHERS HAVE TO SAY.

BUILD LOYALTY AND BECOME LOYAL. This happens as we keep our word. And also as we fight anything that is abusive, unfair, or immoral for our brethren. And also as we work to make our brethren the best disciples they can be.

PROVIDE AND RECEIVE HONEST FEEDBACK. The Scripture teaches us that by speaking the truth to each other in love, we help one another grow into Christ's image (Ephesians 4:15-16). The Lord uses those He sets us with in the local church to help us see ourselves better for the purpose of causing growth. Christians are accountable to one another. Ephesians 5:21 says, *"Submit to one another out of reverence for Christ."* This area of providing honest feedback is a difficult one. It can result in hurt feelings unless we are motivated by love – unless our intentions are pure. We need to perfect our abilities to give and to receive feedback for the church to function properly. The ideal we strive to achieve for giving useful feedback is to see each other as God sees us, which requires we be *"pure in heart."* See Matthew 5:8. When a brother or sister provides this feedback, use it as an opportunity for growth. It's not meant to be an ambush. To enable us to better give and receive honest feedback, we should develop a heart-to-heart relationship with the brethren. Then, because we are perceived as "caring" rather than "critical", we are better able to fulfill the "one another" NT scriptures to help each other grow in Christ.

BUILD COOPERATION AND THE FEELING OF "FAMILY."

COMMUNICATE WELL AND BE ORGANIZED.

DEVELOP A HEART IN OTHERS FOR SERVING.

BUILD OTHERS UP, ENCOURAGE AND EMPOWER THEM

NEVER TAKE OTHERS FOR GRANTED BUT RATHER RECOGNIZE AND REWARD THEM FOR DESERVING SERVICE.

CHRISTIAN EDUCATION STARTS IN THE LOCAL CHURCH

As Great Commission believers, we are called to make disciples. This means we are called to be educators. Jesus said, *"Therefore go and make disciples of all nations ...teaching them to obey everything I have commanded you."* Matthew 28: 19-20 NIV. There's an area of Christian education that can be easily forgotten – that we are partners with the Lord and each other in helping each other mature as Christians. We are partners in the process of helping each other to be shaped into the image of Christ. Ephesians 4:16 NIV says, *"From Him the whole body, joined and held together by every supporting ligament, grows and builds itself up in love, as each part does its work."*

Here's a way to test yourself on how well you're doing as a "growth partner" of the brethren. As you look up the scripture references, ask the Holy Spirit to help you in your "weak" areas. Rate yourself this way: 1 – Strongly Disagree 2- Disagree 3 – Slightly Agree 4 – Agree 5 – Strongly Agree

- I bear with other Christians' personalities and habits by remembering "there but for the grace of God go I." (EPH 4:2) Remember the words of Jesus in JN 13: 14, *"If I then, your Lord and Master, have washed your feet; ye also ought to wash one another's feet."* Rating____
- Even when my brother or sister in Christ is clearly wrong in what they've said or done, I try hard to tell them in a way that keeps the unity of the Spirit in the bond of peace (EPH 4:2). Rating____

- I consider myself to be incomplete without the fellowship of my brothers and sisters in Christ and therefore speak the truth to them (EPH 4:25). Rating____
- I am kind to other Christians, by getting to know them well enough to be sensitive and not hurt them (EPH 4:32). Rating____
- I don't hold grudges. I am not hard-hearted. When I see they regret what they did, I forgive them in the same manner as God, for Christ's sake, forgives me (EPH 4:32). Rating____
- I submit myself as an instrument in God's hand in order to help my brothers and sisters in Christ – even if there's the possibility of being hurt or misunderstood by them. If that makes me feel uncomfortable and humble at times, I do it anyway (EPH 5:21). Also remember *"...that we may be able to comfort them which are in any trouble, by the comfort wherewith we ourselves are comforted of God."* (2COR 1:4) Rating____
- I am consistent and diligent in praying for other Christians (JA 5:16). Rating____
- I serve my brothers and sisters in Christ by faithfully using the gifts God has given me. (GAL 4:13, RO 12:4-9) Rating____
- If my brethren are overtaken in a fault, and seem to be sliding off the track, I don't ignore them but try to restore them, being sensitive to the Holy Spirit's leading (GAL 6:1). Rating____
- Though it costs me time, energy, and money, I bear my brother's or sister's burden. (GAL 6:2). Rating____
- My care for all the brethren is the same. In this way I really practice unity (1COR 12:25-26). Everyone in the kingdom of God should know what to expect – that help will always be there when he/she needs it. Rating____
- I try to prefer others over myself. I am in fellowship with others so I know their needs. I am not just concerned about my own needs, but I make every effort to provide for the needs of others – even the lowliest of the brethren (PH 2:3-4, RO 12:16). Rating____
- I don't make "deals" with Christians or with God (like Jacob in GEN 28:20). I don't make others feel they "owe" me anything.

And I don't let others make me feel that way about them. I remember, however, that I am obligated to love the brethren. (RO 13:8). Rating____

- I avoid judging my brethren. Instead, I'm careful not to make them feel they should do something that they really don't believe they should do. (RO 14:12-13, 23). Rating____
- I make a point to faithfully build up and encourage the brethren (RO 14:19-20). Also see Proverbs 10: 11, 20, 21 that have two constants: A righteous man and words that nourish and refresh others. Let us get a reputation like Job got, *"Thy words have upholden him that was falling, and thou hast strengthened the feeble knees."* (Job 4:4). Rating____
- I am not prejudice. I accept all brethren equally (RO 15:7, JA 2:1). Rating____
- I study the Word of God in order to be able to help instruct and even admonish my brethren when necessary (COL 3:16). Rating____

In our role as a Christian educator and "growth partner", let's remember that our actions speak volumes about what we really believe. And also, let's not focus our energy so much on the masses as we do on one brother or sister at a time. Remember our Lord's words in MT 25:40, *"...Inasmuch as ye have done it unto one of the least of these my brethren, ye have done it unto me."* Jesus never let the masses dissuade or discourage Him from helping people one by one. In LK 8:40, the multitude pressed about Him. Yet in verses 41-56, we read that He took time to minister to one man and one woman in need (i.e. Jairus and the woman with the issue of blood). Jesus calls us to do the same. Let's do what we can to help others - one person at a time. Let God then, as we mature in Christ, add others as we *"seek first the kingdom of God and His righteousness."*

CHRISTIAN EDUCATION FOR THE LOCAL CHURCH

In the last 32 years, I've belonged to seven churches of different denominations, taught the Word of God in six, and been a key note speaker/workshop leader for various Christian organizations. I've found that there's a teaching void in local churches about the following issues: **How does the church work? What do we commit ourselves to do and become? What are our responsibilities to help make it work properly?**

Christians, who consider membership in a local church, need to be educated from the very beginning about what membership means - in order to fulfill God's Word as well as to avoid destructive confrontation and maintain the unity of the Spirit in the bond of peace (Ephesians 4:3). Local churches have different personalities and character. Each may take different approaches to these issues. But each one needs to be clear about a member's commitments and responsibilities to that church. Here's just the "tip of the iceberg" I believe must be taught EARLY…

We all need to know that the foundation of our faith is the Lordship of Jesus Christ (Matthew 16:16-19). As a result of receiving Jesus as Lord, life on our own terms is over. We are obedient to His Word. Good works come as our response to His love for us – and that's how we measure our faith (i.e. by our labor for Him). We develop relationships in the Body based upon a loving commitment to meet each other's needs. We move from isolation into a shared life.

Everybody is accepted as somebody special in the church! We are all ambassadors of Christ! Everyone is accepted as they are while our Lord shapes us into what He wants us to become. Since we are being transformed into His image, church members should be asked EARLY to proactively receive from the ministries of the church and its leadership what is needed for that growth. The local church should clearly ask members to practice those things that will cause this transformation to take place. Therefore, if there is something that needs to be corrected, it may be necessary for church leaders to offer members some loving advice.

How is the church managed? Who is in authority? Where does that authority come from? What's expected of a church member in relation to the church authority? Being a member of the Body means following the leaders God gives us as they follow Christ (Ephesians 4:11). The church is governed by God ruling through His designated, delegated authority. This authority includes the pastor, who is selected by a selection Board appointed by the church. The pastor becomes the Chairman of a Board of Deacons, elected by the church membership. In addition to the pastor and Board there are heads of ministries in the church, usually appointed by the pastor. Authority, however, emanates from relationship. The success of a leader depends very much upon his ability to love, care, and relate to his people. The leaders God gives us can only exercise authority as people voluntarily submit (1Thessalonians 5:12-13). Submission is always voluntary.

How do church members resolve disputes with other church members, board members, and the pastor? Disagreements are to be expected in a church family. They don't happen to hurt or offend anybody, but rather as an opportunity for both people to grow and be shaped into the image of Christ. In accordance with our Lord's instructions in Matthew 18, we are to meet privately with the person and explain what they did to hurt us or what we are disputing about. If it can be resolved at that stage, nothing further is required. It is also acceptable for the two people to "agree to disagree" about something and pray about it. If the matter cannot be resolved, we should ask another church member to meet with us and the other person to resolve the matter. If that doesn't work, we should ask a board member to help resolve the matter. Finally, if that doesn't work, we should involve the pastor. Whatever is decided at that stage should be accepted by both parties. If the dispute is with a board member or the pastor, take another board member to the second confrontation. And if the dispute is with the pastor, the final authority should be at one level higher than the pastor (e.g. district leader).

How does the church keep disputes of any kind to a minimum? Encourage all church members to be open and honest in their relationships rather than burying their true feelings. Insist that when Christians express those feelings they do it with the love of the Lord (Ephesians 4:15). We need to remember His love for us in that while we were still sinners, He died for us (Romans 5:8). Encourage church members to keep their lives connected to Christ through equal measures of Bible Study, Prayer, Worship, Fellowship, Service, and Comforting Others. Provide opportunities to do these things through church services and ministries. Have church members embrace Christ's values to *"put on the mind of Christ."* Also, emphasize that we must stay ready – by proper thoughts and actions - to meet the Lord at any time.

"BELIEVER LEADERS" LEARN, WORSHIP, AND FELLOWSHIP TOGETHER

For many years, I was responsible for developing supervisors who would mentor their people. Now, as President of New Jersey Christian Ministries (NJCM), the Lord has given us instructors and exhibitors who mentor Convention attendees and provide them the latest resources in almost every area of Christian ministry. What a privilege and awesome responsibility to give Christians instruction in God's Word, who then pass it on to others!

Many Christians are unaware of their importance to the Lord. Do you realize, for example, that you are the Lord's leader? There are many different types of leaders: workplace supervisors, pastors, deacons, husbands and wives, parents and grandparents, teachers and coaches. Are you one of them? Then you are a leader. Are you a Christian believer? Then you are Christ's ambassador, an officer in the army of the Lord! And you've been given the Great Commission (Matthew 28: 18-20) by our Lord to go and make disciples of all nations - to lead others to Christ and help them become mature believers. So you too are a leader.

At our annual conventions, 70-90 instructors teach over 100 workshops and help mentor "believer leaders" (like you & me) in the details of such areas as: *Children and Youth Ministries*, *Bible and Theology*, *End Times*, *Spiritual Life*, *Balanced Ministry*, *Church Leadership*, *Marriage and Family*, *The Attack Against Christianity in America, Counseling, Gender Issues*, *Media and Technology*, *Biblical Finances, Cross Cultural and Urban Issues*, and *other creative ministries*. In this article, I'd like to give you some <u>general qualities of Christlike leaders</u> that we can demonstrate in these and other ministry areas, and wherever we are in life and in the Church.

The mantle garment, also translated as "cloak", worn by all God's prophets, helps us understand what's needed to effectively develop the people entrusted to us – children, spouses, teams, church members, other believers or unbelievers. It was a sleeveless garment made from the skins of animals with the hair left on it. See 2 Kings 2:12-14. The mantle helps us know what's needed for people to be productive, empowered, and creative, who "live by faith" and who take responsibility and feel accountable for their actions. It will show us how to "free" our people to be all they can be in their roles as employees, church members, children and grandchildren, students, Christian believers, etc. Jesus clearly demonstrated these same qualities and behaviors for us to emulate. Here are some things the mantle shows us:

The mantle served the prophet, it wasn't served - so our attitude as leaders is one of servant-leader. In John 13, Jesus washed the feet of His disciples. He then told them (and us) to wash one another's feet - to do as He had shown them. He said that they would be happy if they did this. Jesus said the greatest person in the kingdom of God is the servant of all.

The mantle also provided warmth for the prophet. We leaders need to give our people the warmth of knowing that they are our greatest asset and highest concern. We need to take the time (like Jesus always did) to get to know them and let them know us. God came in the flesh to show us who He was - to gain a heart-to-heart commitment from us. We leaders need to build a heart-to-heart relationship with those entrusted to us.

The mantle also provided protection from the elements. It couldn't have holes that would let the rain in or be so thin that it gave no resistance to the wind. It needed to have "**integrity**." As the prophet depended upon his mantle and gained confidence in what it could do, so our people need to be able to depend upon our sound judgment and wisdom from above. James 3:17 tells us that this wisdom means among other things having pure motives, being compassionate with failure, and gaining respect by being fair, genuine, and keeping our word.

A mantle isn't able to "push" anything - a cloth garment has no pushing power. It can, however, be tied around something and pull it. We leaders need to have this "pull power" - like Jesus Christ. He always says things like *"follow me"* (John 12:26), and *"come unto me"* (Matthew 11:28). By our behaviors that come from embracing the "mantle" leadership qualities, we should send this message to our people: "Follow me as I follow Christ in leadership". All believers need to have this "pull power" to attract the lost, unite believers, and disciple each other. In these last days, all believers need to be Christlike leaders willing to tie themselves to others in the process of discipleship - to be ready to lead as the Lord brings the harvest of new believers into our churches. Don't leave that work to the pastors and deacons alone.

Let's be the Lord's "believer leaders" and emulate His leadership qualities. Whenever we're being taught, let's maintain a "new wineskin" heart – one that will stretch as the Lord pours His truth into us.

Topical Index

Jesus Hasting To Suffer[8]

The Saviour, - what a noble flame
Was kindled in his breast,
When, hasting to Jerusalem,
He marched before the rest!

With all his sufferings full in view,
And woes to us unknown,
Forth to the task his spirit flew;
T'was love that urged him on.

Lord, while thy bleeding glories here
Engage our wondering eyes,
We learn our lighter cross to bear,
And hasten to the skies.

---

[8] William Cowper, 1890

Topical Index

www.ingramcontent.com/pod-product-compliance
Lightning Source LLC
LaVergne TN
LVHW090945080826
845145LV00003B/894

* 9 7 8 0 9 7 5 3 7 8 6 1 8 *